ECHOES *of the*
Cosmic Song

Leaves from an Occult Notebook

by MARY GRAY

MARGENT PRESS
New York · 1945

COPYRIGHT, 1945, BY RICHARD R. SMITH

PUBLISHED BY MARGENT PRESS
120 EAST 39TH STREET, NEW YORK 16, N. Y.

*All rights reserved. No part of this book may be repro-
duced in any form without permission of the publisher.*

BOOKS IN WARTIME

The War Production Board has curtailed the use of book paper. In compliance with the Board's ruling this book is printed on a lighter weight paper and with smaller margins than were conventional in peace times.

The publisher feels, however, that the slimmer volume which has been produced is more convenient to hold and to read; and it has the added merit of saving labor, paper and type metal.

SET UP BY BROWN BROTHERS LINOTYPERS
PRINTED IN THE UNITED STATES OF AMERICA
BY THE FERRIS PRINTING COMPANY

GLOSSARY

ADEPT
: Fully initiated Being who watches over humanity.

AUGOEIDES
: The divine self of man.

CHELA
: An aspirant or disciple.

DEMONS
: Entities belonging to another more primitive evolution having a necessary destructive role in cosmos.

DEVA
: Belonging to the angelic world.

DHARMA
: The law of duty.

ELEMENTAL
: Beings of etheric bodies not usually visible, some created by men; some the lower evolving forms of the angelic world.

GREAT WATCHER *or* SILENT WATCHER
: An exalted Being from another evolution who is the court of appeal in an emergency on the Planet.

KAMA MANAS
: The lower mind motivated by passion.

KARMA
: The law of retribution—cause and effect.

KUMARA
: Advanced Being from Venus sent to take over the governing of this planet in the middle of the third Root Race.

KUNDALINI
: Life running through centres in man.

MAHA CHOHAN
: Head of organizing ray of Hierarchy.

MANAS
: The intellectual principle which differentiates man the thinker.

MANU
: The spiritual father of a Race.

MONAD
: The divine spark to whom man is attached.

PLANETARY LOGOS
: The Lord of the Planet.

RAKSHASA
: Beings active on the destructive side of life.

ROOT RACE
: One of seven great ages in life of Planet. Each Root Race has a main continent later destroyed to give place to new land elsewhere.

CONTENTS

7

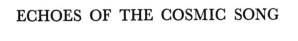

ECHOES OF THE COSMIC SONG

COSMIC HOSTS

Through the highways and the byways
Of the vaster Cosmic Scheme,
In the sunlight—in the starlight,
Come and go a golden stream.

Host on Host from distant coast,
Fringes of the Cosmic deep,
Golden, gleaming, star mists streaming,
Pace they on, their watch to keep.

We small mortals, at the portals
Of a system far unfurled,
Catch but flashes, tidal washes,
From ancient star and distant world.

We are blind and cannot find
The key to all of Life's Great Story;
Until we rise with open eyes,
We cannot know its Untold Glory!

FOREWORD

These excerpts from a notebook on meditation, kept during the years 1927 through 1929, make no claim to authority. They offer the student of philosophy and occultism outlines of a new pattern of thought about the history of our planet. For some they may give answer to deep-lying queries as to the purpose and the plan for our humanity, its problems and the causes of our anguish here. Others may find strange and intriguing ideas cast up like unusual shells on a lonely beach. But what follows will be better understood if certain basic tenets of philosophy are accepted as foundation stones upon which the plan is built.

These premises are found in some form in all religions.

First, man is divine in spirit, the son of God the Father, who through experience here unfolds his latent powers.

Second, there is a spiritual evolution for which physical evolution exists, that ever more evolved forms may be prepared to serve the unfolding powers of the divine spirit in man.

Third, there is a law of justice which governs our destiny, a promise of achievement through our own efforts if we strive for that fulfillment. "As ye sow, so shall ye reap." Man is thus the arbiter of his own fate.

Fourth, between humanity and the ultimate God exist many Beings of varying powers and varying degrees of spiritual potency. In Christianity we hear of the seven Spirits before the throne, of Angels and Archangels, of

13

Thrones, Dominations, Princedoms, Virtues, Powers, and these superior Beings as shown by the evidence of many different scriptures play their part in the plan for humanity. And as there are beneficent angels, so also there are demons who are injurious and hostile to man.

On the path to divinity man must learn to choose between good and evil and there are therefore inevitably those who stand for the light, the upward path to conscious union with God. And there are also those who rebel and seek to win the kingdoms of the earth for themselves, who represent thereby spiritual evil in high places—the Lords of the Dark Face who seek to dominate man for their own selfish glory and power.

From the pages which follow, a warp of strange destiny will appear upon which the shuttle of our human life moves. In the veil of mystery that shrouds our earth, rents appear through which we gain glimpses of a strange and terrible story, one that explains the phrase "born in sin." Milton's fallen angels appear and the doom uttered when man was driven from Eden is heard.

Furthermore, it is premised that every planet has its own evolving humanity, not perhaps in bodies like ours, but in those suited to their own planetary environment. Not only our planets, but the whole cosmic scheme with its suns, stars, constellations and attendant planets are part of one great cosmic plan whereby ever-increasing expansion of consciousness occurs. Gautama the Buddha said, "Veil after veil will lift, but veil after veil remains." Throughout the vast realms of manifested worlds there exist possible relationships of sister stars and Systems, of interlocking evolutions and rulers. Our Great Father is the spiritual Being who has erected our solar System. The Father of any humanity should be the indwelling Spirit of the planet, the Lord who uses our planet as his outer vesture.

In our era there has been a cosmic failure and humanity has become thereby the Great Orphan.

PROLOGUE

PROLOGUE

ANGELIC HOSTS OF THE DAWN

Far away where the stars are sweeping, where the winds of space are breathing their age-long melody, far away on the rim of known creation, there dwell the Angelic Hosts of the Dawn. From age to age, from planet to planet, as the hour comes for the presaging of new light, they come, flaunting their banners in the Eastern sky, a myriad host of Holy Ones, who herald the light. Their lesser followers carry from eon to eon the symbol of the dawn in the colours of the returning sun. But the true dawn, of which this upon our planet is but a dim reflection, represents the reopening of life in the cycle of God's incarnations. That resplendent and majestic hour is symbolized throughout eternity by the splendour of dawn, by the ever-returning wonder of it in men's hearts, by the ever-renewed yearning for it in times of doubt, darkness or distress. Peace.

MESSENGERS OF GOD

Peace. See you not the forerunners of change, the Herald Angels of the new day? Can you not feel in the very atmosphere of your world the changes which are being wrought? Day by day in this new world the Angelic Hosts are marshalling their forces and seeking entry through every opening, through every crack and crevice, whereby the faintest beam of light may pass. As man begins to recover from the shock of the trials which lie behind him, as he

19

permits himself once more to respond to the holy and joyous harmonies of the inner worlds, he will find his mind opening to new understanding of the truth—or, you might say, new truths. They are not new. Truth stands majestic and immortal, eternal and unchangeable, but the mind perceives it from new angles of vision, from greater heights and depths, with deeper understanding. One may cognate a truth with the mind, but one does not truly know it until, like a great light, it has irradiated one's whole being, one's whole consciousness on every plane. Prophets seek to expand the avenues of consciousness. They are but teachers of the spiritual world seeking to unfold the knowledge suited to each grade, as the classes mature and progress. In our day, more and more are capable of entering and learning from the advanced classes. This marks the progress of humanity —the ever-increasing number who can enter and share the wisdom of the spiritual groups, who can live the life of the vision made manifest in action.

Oh, ye peoples of the Planet, the Darkened Star, look up. Seek to open the gates that the dawn may enter—that the Light of the Spiritual Sun may illumine your world.

Time moves. The end of darkness approaches. Make ready the highways of understanding for the holy footprints of the Messengers of God. Peace.

PEACE

There is peace in the silence of the heart when it reaches inward to its God. The solitary peace, known to the solitary heart, alone can be real. All other peace must pass, for it is established upon duality on the planes of form where impermanence remains.

In the days of the future, more will be revealed. The pattern of the great tapestry of the Solar System is but just unrolling its first designs. The time has come when man may be entrusted with some of the greater secrets which have heretofore been withheld lest in his ignorance he should misuse the knowledge or misinterpret it to his undoing.

Knowledge will be vouchsafed as the mind absorbs the information already accorded.

Peace. This is the most precious possession of the human heart. It should be treasured, and never lost, since only in the sanctuary of peace within the heart can the light of God shine. So can be illumined all problems of life, as the power of peace, the tranquillity of inner stillness is applied. There is a power in the peace of the heart which confounds all evil. It is the source of control over man and beast, elemental, and djinn. The mountains represent peace, the sea, action.

When the mirror of the mind is stilled, upon its shining surface appear reflections of the coming splendours of the coming Age. Serenity must be achieved in every department of life, in every phase of being. As action rises from serenity, so is it efficient and powerful. The haste of our minds alone causes impatience, irritation, weariness and strain. Peace, the inner peace of the spirit, must abide always with us, and about us, and inspire all our actions.

The hurry-skurry of the body and the hurry-skurry of the mind are foes to peace. Let them cease. Tranquil, fair and courteous be all speech, all thought, all action.

Invoke the presence of peace, Oh ye seekers after truth. Invoke the spirit of peace, all ye seekers after vision or inspiration. Invoke the power of peace, all ye servers of the

Law who carry on the outcome of the Law in manifestation. Peace.

Spiritual Insight.—The peace of God dwells in the heart of those who renounce life. He who loseth his life shall find it. Peace enters into the heart which puts aside worldly desire and lives in the Kingdom within. In all things there is compensation.

The Gateways of the Kingdom are narrow and the soul who passes into them must be quit of mortal desire and freed from the elemental forces which rise in the vehicles as a result of the animal heredity; forces which have much of value and use in the earlier days of evolution and which perhaps are the only means whereby reluctant flesh can be made to tread the arduous paths of self-sacrifice. But even mother instinct which protects the race at its inception and which builds in man and in woman alike the desire to protect the weak of its own people—this instinct which is the basis of all unselfishness and sacrifice in the early stages of life becomes a menace to the freedom of the soul in the later stages of evolution. It binds man or woman to the life of form, to the sacrifice of all things to protect form. It has in it the whole elemental impulse to protect and cling to form —even if that form belongs to another, whether it is one's own progeny or the young of the race. It teaches untold sacrifice that the form may continue. But when the higher law comes into power, all regard for the form must cease. One must free oneself of trammels of all elemental essence and reach upward to the flame of spirit which finds its expression in the formless worlds, which rise above the limitations of earth life into the free essence of the pure spirit. This is now the next great lesson before the race, the disregard of form in the personal life; the domination of life from the spiritual centre, from the formless plane, which is man's true heritage and where lies his Kingdom.

To achieve this, instinct must be torn away as trappings from a mummy on the day of resurrection according to the ideas of ancient Egypt. And instinct which has guided the race through its early evolution, taught and trained it, must give way to spiritual insight into man's evolutionary path and future goal. Through spiritual insight only can the next great chasm be bridged in man's upward path to the heritage he lost, the garden of Eden where he dwelt in the formless worlds.

The Mysteries.—The unveiling of the great truths which are being revealed must await the appointed hour.

Throughout the ages the mysteries have sought gradually to prepare men's minds for the truths which planetary and racial evolution would force upon them. The time has now come when evolution is unveiling scientific secrets of the utmost menace to the race if unsuitably used. To counterbalance these a group of occult truths are being given through various channels which will build up a group of thinkers and occultly trained minds which can cope successfully with the problems of civilization which are arising. Students of the occult may not be good business men and women, but they are trained on the inner planes into a powerful band who carry their influence far. On the inner planes they are trained occultists. The time is now approaching when that knowledge of the use of occult forces to accomplish the purposes of man must come in part at least into the lower brain. The mysteries are to be established and Isis will again speak through her neophytes and seers as of old in Egypt.

I · THE KARMIC LAW

I · THE KARMIC LAW

KARMA, DHARMA AND KISMET

The Greater Plan.—The far-flung realms of the Cosmic Rulers lie like islands and continents in the sea of space. Each of these realms has a Ruler, a lesser Lord, who reports to his Overlord at appointed periods. These realms are governed by their Rulers with freedom as far as may be, within certain laws which are the lines and axes of unfoldment laid down by the Greater Plan within which the lesser must unfold. Call the systematic laws Karma, and the solar interpretation Dharma, and there comes a better understanding of the working of these laws. Kismet is interpreted as Fate. It is actually the superlaw which governs alike both man and planet. Treating humanity as a whole, as a group of cells closely connected with the planet, and existing as part of the Solar System, this group is subject to periodic changes, to periodic flux and flow of the vital energies.

Cleansing of the System.—These periodic changes involve humanity as a whole and can be foreseen to some extent by seers. Sometimes the wiping out of great sections of humanity are necessary for the cleansing of the System. The fate of those involved is not Dharmic but Karmic; not resulting from their own debts but because they fall under the great Karmic law of the System, which acts on groups rather than on units. Whole nations fall under the Karmic equation; and men share the Karma of their nation. If

27

for special reasons some nation must be preserved, this devolves upon the individual effort of the Ruler of the Planet or the Genius of the Race or the Manu and His Group.

Planetary Destruction.—Occasionally a great planetary destruction is necessary to wipe out ancient bodies, to make way for a newer and better type. Then rise great destroyers who sweep over nations and destroy, such as Genghis Khan. They are driven by Karmic law, not planetary forces.

The car of Attila was driven by Karmic necessity, as was the chariot of the Kings of Egypt. In great issues man is but a puppet who must follow the Dharma of life, even if it seems in direct opposition to the forces of evolution. Again, it may well be the role that the planetary Dharma requires.

In the saga of Arjuna, each man's duty is clear and necessary. The great battle could not be avoided, for the barrier of Kshattriyas, the warrior caste, had to be swept away to open the spiritual treasures of India to the world. Human emotions, fear, desire, hatred, are roused by the Devas of each race to prepare men for the necessary debacle which Karma requires. If a man fulfill his duty and his role to the best of his ability, he aids the Plan.

Somewhat of the same thing was done in the Great War, which destroyed so large a portion of the ruling classes—the aristocrats—to make way for democracy.

In Russia it was accomplished otherwise, and so again in China. But the purpose was the same, the purging of the planet of cells which were clogging progress, the wiping away of bodies unfitted for the new era. The fate of the individual was unimportant. It was the wholesale destruction that was needed.

Sometimes this is brought about by filling an individual

with the fire of genius and fanaticism; sometimes by on-sets of destructive groups from outside who act like a poison and force the system to elimination. It was this latter in the Great War. But poisons are dangerous and may kill as well as cure. In such a case the organism is too weak to be worth saving. It is well to remember the parallel between the body of humanity and that of the individual.

There are other periods when lesser sacrifices are neces-sary for the ultimate good. Then individuals have pressure put upon them until they can endure no more, and through some elemental force, ambition, fear, greed, etc., are com-pelled to act in a savage manner—the Inquisition, the mas-sacre on St. Bartholomew's Eve. Curiously enough, those chosen for carrying out such tragedies are those capable of courage, sacrifice, fearlessness; all qualities suited to heroes as well as to villains. They are usually capable of being aroused to fanaticism and do not fear public opinion.

THE LAW OF FEAR AND THE LAW OF LOVE

Fear.—There are many strange currents at work in this planet. The whole strange tale is not revealed. Certain fundamental errors have occurred, followed by far-reaching Karmic results, and the effects of those continue in ever-widening circles, like the ripples of a pool when disturbed by a falling stone.

The true mystery cannot yet be fully unveiled. But cer-tain it is that those involved in human incarnation, by the very conditions which surround them, constantly incur fresh Karmic debts which make the total hard to pay in full. Since the immediate descent of Karma in full upon all would hold back evolution for considerable periods, there are those who repair the damage wrought by man; and by continuing their abode here after having completed the required evolutionary cycle, steadily transmute some of the evil created by ignorance and fear. Most evil is born of one or of the other—ignorance of the law, and indifference, or fear for oneself. Fear is the great and terrible curse laid upon humanity, and its reflexes are far-reaching. That is why educators and others seek to remove fear from consciousness, but the subconscious effect of past ages is so great that it must not be removed too rapidly until other curbing forces have supplanted it. It is a matter of delicate adjustment between one force and the other.

Love.—The law of fear must still govern certain undisciplined and undeveloped natures; but the law of love and co-operation must as rapidly as possible be applied to all who can respond to it. We are yet in the grip of titanic and elemental forces loose upon the planet. The savage rites of some of the early religions in the Americas have left powerful thought forms and evil conditions which affect the new, more sensitive psychic types. They revert to the cruelty in which these lands have indulged in past times. This is the immediate cause of many horrible cases of crime for which it is hard to account otherwise. Human motives hark back into the bosom of time and rise frequently from past breaches of law. Possibly man and animals were not intended to materialize their bodies so densely but the drift of matter away from the spiritual poles brought this about, and they have taken on in the physical vehicles traits which belong only to the torturers who were planned to work in finer matter, not on physical but on emotional and on mental planes. It is to be remembered that doom was announced and man cast from Eden—to live on earth because he broke the law. He passed from the finer planes to physical bodies, and animals followed him, since they must shape their evolution to his. Thus came pain, murder and death and hatred, fear and cruelty. Gradually, by pain, the bodies, the physical elementals, are losing their grip upon humans, permitting their escape. One main reason for abstaining from meat eating is to make this escape easier.

Development of Intelligence.—The vibrations of fear are powerful upon this planet, and must be modified. There has been cause for fear in the past, and its influence has come down through the ancient folk tales and fables.

There are terrible deposits of fear on the planet, great grey accumulations that rise like vapours from a marsh and throttle the soul. When one considers that fear is almost the strongest instinct in nature—the one upon which self-preservation depends, it is evident what a hold it has upon humanity. It has been through fear that intelligence has developed. It is still the most potent force on the planet. Nor is its purpose completed. It must still serve in many ways.

Fear is peculiar, in that it paralyzes man for a time and yet intensifies the pressure on the intellect, when the fear is not too immediate. Then it often paralyzes the intellect as well.

ELEMENTAL FORCES MUST BE CONTROLLED

The Power of Will.—The power of will can scarcely be measured. It is the manifestation of the Godhead. Without it, man remains a puppet of elemental forces. The energy of lower classes of evolution, vegetable, animal and savage, is based upon elemental force over which they have no control. Fear, desire, anger, greed, hunger, pleasure all exert their sway over the savage man. It is because of the danger of yielding to these elemental forces that the Catholic church has listed the deadly sins. The elemental forces must be controlled before man can emerge into the powers of divinity. No force which controls a man's reason can be anything but detrimental, after a certain point of evolution is passed.

Desire Must Be Conquered.—All these forces act through the Karmic elemental and its associate, the cunning Kama Manas or Manas roused to action by elemental pressures. Desire is said to be the lower aspect of will, but only insofar as it rouses energy and action and thought, and so governs the life. Actually, it must be conquered ere will can truly manifest. Desire rouses the whole nature to action, and thereby draws down a simulacrum of will, but will can only act in pure manifestation when the whole lower nature has become subordinate and controlled and no longer at the mercy of any elemental force.

Take note: Ambition is a form of greed—raised to a high point in Kama Manas. Fear is the source of convention, obedience to authority, mass consciousness. Passion is the elemental desire linked to the body in action and supplemented by desire for possession. Only that love which is freed from elemental action can be truly divine. Anger is linked to pride, both elemental forces, one of power, one of self-protection.

The Perfect Balance.—The occulist must rise above all elemental forces and, moved by compassion, use his awakened and dominant will for the service of humanity. It is this perfect balance, unmoved by fear, greed, desire, pride, prejudice, that at last frees man from the clay of his human heritage.

II · THE SOLAR SYSTEM

II · THE SOLAR SYSTEM

How Established.—Through the various methods of evolution of different humanities upon different planets, the composite forces of a Solar System are established. The Solar Logos encompasses great groups of entities within His aura, and brings them into obedience to His will, wisdom and commands, but they are no more part of Him in actual fact than relatives or clans are an integral part of the chief of that family. In the case of a Logos, when his Consciousness has become great enough to encompass the needs and supervise the actions of the hosts comprising a Solar System, He summons to His assistance from His past or from related Systems, His chief assistants. Those closest to Him are usually souls who have proved themselves by individual association in the past.

Qualifications for Logoi.—When He chooses His chief subordinates, He puts into their care certain great departments of the Solar System, and responsibility for the manipulation of certain great reservoirs of power which He has been gathering through many eons for His great task. In every incarnation He has put aside some portion of the engendered force for future needs. This often imposes hardships upon the physical life as less force is available for use to accomplish the rather minor purposes of one life and, therefore, greater effort is needed and a great strain is put upon the vehicles.

But in the end, vast accumulations result. He actually

35

draws off the powers of the vehicles through pressure of one kind or another into reservoirs. Some is acquired through endurance of great pain and agony of mind and body, some through joy and intense aspiration, some through intense intellectual efforts. Physical pain and physical exertion create reservoirs of power over material and physical forces. Gradually, He forces one vehicle after another to distil from the Universal Essence the forces peculiar to itself and to exert its powers to the last degree until it is literally squeezed dry, so that He may have the maximum of power in the reservoirs of which any vehicle is capable.

Only those who are capable of terrific exertions of will and terrific endurance can in any way qualify for Logoi. The path is arduous. It is easier to qualify for subordinate positions, to achieve power within limited spheres, to supervise only limited and specialized groups.

Call for Volunteers.—A long time ago, when the time had come for a new System, word was flashed to a large group of related suns and their planets, calling for volunteers for various posts. The Solar Systems are not created by the individual Solar Logoi, but by the greater Logoi, the sphere or centre of their greater orbit, which has reached the need for further expression and development. Before this time has fully arrived, They announce the approaching need and call for candidates. The work to be done is laid out in great archetypal plans, flashed into the great central chamber of the greater System, and heliographed into the sacred central chamber of each Hierarchy upon each planet connected with that System.

These plans show how the work is to be done and the qualities required for each position, graded according to ray, power and hierarchical position. Certain Monads determine to try to qualify for given positions. They then determine by careful study where they can best develop the powers needed, and at once take incarnation in those planets. This accounts for certain "sports" which appear in all humanities, more especially on our planet, where the conditions permit intensive training, though in an excessively difficult way. Also, such tough vehicles are developed here to meet the extraordinary conditions that great quantities of force can be specialized through them, as they have extraordinary endurance and resistance to pressure. One can develop a higher temperature with safety in a tough metal container than in glass.

A Logos Establishes His Claim.—When a Logos establishes his claim, he calls the volunteers for the other positions and appoints them according to capacity and personal loyalty. This last is highly important. Only those who have proved themselves able to work well together can be safely chosen. The greater unit of the governing group comprised of lesser ones must show enough homogeneous qualities to assure harmony. This is often best assured by intense personal attachment and the proved capacity to work as one under a given head.

Lord of Our Chain.—In the case of this Solar System, this personal affection was not enough emphasized and its importance not enough realized. The great Being chosen for the post of Lord of our Chain was of stupendous intellectual power, but not closely enough linked to our Logos. He was chosen for capacity and not for personal association. The result was so disastrous that warning has gone forth from one end of the Sirian System to the other. He considered himself wiser than his Leader and refused to accept the Leader's ruling in the domain over which he, the subordinate, had charge. Disaster resulted, and when the planet became leaderless and chaotic conditions resulted, thousands of unsatisfied and undisciplined souls rushed in like adventurers. The chaos became worse, and order was re-established only at great sacrifice.

The Dark Planet

The Fallen Angel.—The denizens of the Dark Planet are curious. Their evolution is strange. Yet they have a purpose in the plan. The fallen Angel is our Planetary Logos who sought a kingdom in material matter for himself and his satellites. All those who are shadowed by the planet have intensification of the individuality as their distinguishing mark. It is these who cry loudest for justice, against tyranny, for personal rights, and who'see domination in almost all laws for the good of the social unit which infringes upon the personal liberty of the individual unit.

Volunteers.—When rebellion brought about the disasters which followed the establishment of our chain, help was invoked, for the Logos found the pain existing intolerable and volunteers arrived to help solve the problem. Forces which had been set in motion must be allowed to fulfill themselves. The problem was to short-circuit the danger and the disaster as much as possible. Many who volunteered became blinded and confused in purpose when they entered the planetary bodies with all their original warps and twists. Confusion and panic resulted to the volunteers also. Yet nevertheless good was and will be accomplished. The planetary Logos had drawn about him discontented egos from the whole scheme.

Obedient Souls.—Side by side with the rebels who endangered the Solar System's success, volunteers of obedient temper came in to help balance the others and to work gradually for the reformation of the rebels. Not only did volunteers of a lofty point of evolution come in to throw the power of their influence upon the side of order, but souls about to begin the pilgrimage volunteered to form that great obedient mass of humanity which could respond to ideals and to the call of order. A condition of chaos was the greatest threat, since chaos would permit the rebels to exercise their powers and to sweep others into the turmoil of cruelty and orgy. Hence powerful leaders volunteered to hold the nations individually in check, until the mind through evolution should have developed and order could be recognized by the mass of men as vitally necessary.

This struggle between the forces is exemplified in all religions, the struggle between darkness and light, between Satan and God.

Advisory Board.—That lofty Spirit who sought to give more individual freedom than the law allowed to his kingdom deeply repented of the confusion which arose and sought by every means to allay the pain and suffering that resulted from his folly. He voluntarily abandoned his lofty position, entrusting it to an Advisory Board as it were, summoned from various parts of the System who agreed to carry on the work as best it might be done. He, himself, departed into other regions to work out his error and to liberate forces by intensive labour which might be used to equalize gradually the harm he had done. Thus the planet and chain became "The Poor Orphan" for the close relation which exists between a planetary Logos and his chain under usual conditions was broken. Like an orphaned child who has not its parents' guidance and support during his early years and who suffers from many mistakes and maladies as a result, humanity stumbles onward, calling in vain upon the Father who should protect him, but who is not. Other agents do what they can, but the house falls in disorder when the Master is absent.

In the end, probably great strength and endurance will come to those human souls who achieve alone and who, knowing the doom, have dared enter the Kingdom of Earth.

Slowly the rebels must be won by the intolerable sacrifices of the others. No wonder there is more rejoicing over· one black sheep than over the ninety and nine, for each black sheep so won reduces the heavy responsibility and the load carried by the Board and its assistants; and reduces, too, the danger and the darkness that overshadows the world. It is one more man-eating tiger set at rest.

The Poor Orphan.—When the shadows deepen, know that only within oneself can one find that inner power which makes for light. Reach inward to the Godhead, the great Divinity beyond this temporal sphere. He moves only within the spirit of man. The Father of the planet who should respond is not. He only could give aid in controlling temporal circumstances. He is not. So the poor orphan suffers and agonizes and stumbles blindly on.

Yet help comes from those myriad volunteer souls who carry the light within and who bring with them the memory of radiance and of goodness, and who reach directly through the dark shadows of earth to the eternal. "I and my Father are one." "Who seeth me, seeth the Father." "My burden is light. Come to me, ye who are weary, and I will give you rest." Again, the courageous volunteer, seeking through his own strength and sacrifice and devotion to replace that missing strength of the earthly Father who is not.

Thus confusion came upon the planet. Hence the reason for so many atheists, denying a God who seems powerless. He is powerless; and the greater God can replace him only through the ministrations of His human children, through the hands of man himself. "Pray not to the darkness, nor bribe the helpless Gods. Within yourself deliverance must be sought."

Over all the planet a veil hangs. It is the mist of ignorance which veils the planet from the radiance of the Inner God. This planet has plunged too deep into matter, and her progress upward is painful and slow. Men with their sensitized, imaginative spirits and minds have shared the lot of animals. The impetus of the planetary rebellion overcame some of the laws of attraction and permitted spirit and matter to be too greatly separated and the current or spark passing from one to the other has been dangerously feeble. At times it seemed as if it might cease altogether, the entire planet disintegrate, and the long experiment require to be begun again.

But, due to the titanic effort of the Sons of Men, the cycle turns upward. Slowly the world rolls from the bed of mud into which it has sunk and starts upon its journey toward the light. No wonder the whole System watches and prays. It is the turning point of the terrible struggle.

Many, many who have been the cause of destruction in the past are now lending their efforts to the upward move. Many who have caused confusion and sorrow among the Sons of Light are now lending their powerful co-operation as they learn to reverence the new vision which, at last, after endless sacrifices dawns upon their gaze.

The Darkness Lightens.—Now that the hour has come when the darkness lightens, many have come to assist at the birth of the new spiritual age. Before this, any attempt to help was useless for they could not contact the low planes upon which humanity functioned. Until humanity had raised its consciousness upward it could not grasp the hands reached down to succor it and to lift it upward to the heights. Now that time has come and throughout all the worlds the Hallelujahs ring. Man once again may take his place by his Brothers at his Father's table and share in the glory of His Presence. Alone he has achieved, and alone he has trod the path. Man's praises shall be sounded through all the worlds unto the end of time. Hosanna in the highest and deepest gratitude to all those holy spirits who have shared in the toil and in the victory!

THE GREAT WATCHER

The Silent Watcher.—The Great Watcher corresponds at a high level to the Silent Watcher of a Planetary System or Solar System. When the great catastrophe occurred, it so involved the interlocked Systems that it won attention from most exalted Beings. Dire results threatened if the wreck could not be salvaged. It must be understood that it was not *here* that the catastrophe took place, but upon a most exalted sphere—the War in Heaven, indeed—and the destructive residue of souls, who had shared in the catastrophe, were cast down when their planet or System exploded onto this fiery cinder, here to atone.

Why the Great Watcher Intervened.—Then it was that compassion sought to shorten their doom, and prepared a place for their habitation where they might evolve as humans, howbeit under a heavy doom of pain, and not be cast utterly into the demonic spheres. As before explained, when the planet was prepared for human evolution, innocent souls were added to the group of insurgents to modify the forces here and to profit by the speed of evolution here below. It is because of the Exalted Beings involved in this downfall that the attention of High Lords was drawn to the problem and that the Great Watcher personally intervened.

The Task Accomplished.—His Power played upon the planet like lightning, stirring all into activity, rousing, maddening, destroying, until the whole planet was in ferment, explosive, violent, agitated. Yet, withal, he has had such power that he has controlled and guided the forces loosed and led men up a path of almost impossible steepness, to the edge of the peak of salvation. Once the peak is attained by a certain proportion of the race, he will turn aside, the task accomplished, or so far accomplished as to permit its being entrusted to lesser hands with safety.

THE SOLAR LORDS

Visiting Lords.—In the highest worlds of form connected with this planet, gather the Solar Lords with their retinues. There, too, are the visiting Lords received, with due pomp and ceremony. It is due to the odd and tragic history of our planet that so many from far away come as visitors: and also to the group of Volunteer Lords who are known in their own places, and watched in their work here with deep interest by their earlier associates and friends. It is but natural that this great experiment, like to nothing before seen in the solar realms, should evoke curiosity and speculation.

Overlords.—It is because of humanity's doom, and its strange admixture with demonic influences, that the rulers cannot forecast with assurance what the reaction to any given stimulus will be. It is the great problem of the Overlords—that of distributing forces for humanity's evolution, and yet seeking to direct that force so that it may not be too destructive. Man must be awakened from the lethargies in which he falls by the sheer oppression of physical needs, by the never-ending round of physical duties and efforts which alone assure his life upon this arduous planet. He must be roused to concerted efforts to free himself from the slavery required by the needs of mere livelihood to conquer the natural forces of the world, and become master, not slave. He must be roused to an understanding of his task, his destiny, and his present opportunities; and yet, so limited is his understanding, so perverse his brain, that it can be done only by stirring emotions and ideas that may become very menacing to the welfare of the world. The by-products of rousing a semi-demonic group of humans may be tragic and disastrous. But perhaps more disastrous is the leaving of humans prone in ignorance, darkness and slavery.

Outpouring of Force.—With these delicate problems of adjustment to meet, it is clear that the Solar Lords are taxed to the ultimate point of their resourcefulness. Therefore, when new forces are liberated upon a planet coincident with the new necessary steps in evolution, many of the retinue incarnate to help distribute that force as wisely as possible. Hence it is that when an outpouring of force is directed towards a special country or institution, a group of volunteers at once incarnates there. Even then, there are serious questions to meet, in regard to those very incarna-

tions, for they cannot always take the best bodies in a nation
and the most spiritual but those where influence can be
wielded. Frequently the heredity is so bad that the ego can
manifest but little of its purpose and that often in a dis-
torted fashion. So evolution is a constant gamble on this
planet, and the governors are obliged to check and counter-
check the very forces they have set in motion, as disaster
threatens in one quarter or another.

Souls Incarnate with Purpose.—Hence, one great virtue
is adaptability in an agent, and quick adjustment to changing conditions. Compromise is the law of great rulers. Here
one comes upon an odd problem. Souls are sent into incarnation to accomplish a carefully planned purpose. A vision
is given them of their duty which remains in a fairly fixed
form on the inner planes, and pours down its influence upon
the personality. Good, so far. But in carrying out this vision
a certain amount of intensity of purpose is needed: almost
a fanatical bias. As the great plan unfolds, it is often found
necessary to modify the original plan of the visionary. Can
he be responsive enough to catch the new vision and adjust
to it, or will his fanaticism prevent that and ruin his usefulness?

On the other hand, will he be so responsive that the
cumulative thought power of his era can influence him and
destroy his vision entirely? It is clear what a nice adjustment
is needed. For a man is beset on all sides by forces of heredity within his own nature to meet and conquer—greed,
wrath and lust—lest they destroy him. Likewise, he is subject to the pressure of public opinion from without, and
finally moved by the intensity of his own vision, which may
become obsolete and need to be changed. Is it any wonder

that failures occur and that work progresses slowly! This, too, explains why it is as important to know when to release a plan, as when to seize it. Verily, the Path of Wisdom is as a razor's edge. The Masters themselves are in constant doubt, and seek to gauge the currents in humanity with scrupulous effort.

Relation to First Kumara.—It may be of interest to understand the relations of the Solar Lords to the First Kumara and His assistants. The Kumara is the Regent of the planet in direct touch with humanity. He and his Council and the groups of the Hierarchy and Brotherhood are, as it were, tutors to men. They carry on the actual government of the physical plane, the supervision of physical life and development. But they receive their orders from the Solar Lords, who act as Council for the Dominant Lord during His Incumbency. Each Solar Lord has charge of the distribution of the force of His constellation for the Chain.

The Solar Lords are, in fact, in charge not only of the planet, but of the Chain and series of Chains. In time, it is hoped, that humans and Devas of this planet can supervise the work for Them so far as this planet is concerned, and relieve Them of Their onerous duties.

Beauty of Court in Exile.—The beauty and splendour that surround the Solar Lords who hold court in exile pass belief. Because it is the united effort of many groups come from far-separated realms, and with greatly varying powers, the court becomes a scintillating centre of colour and light, a marvelous mosaic of jewels which attracts the attention of other Systems by the unusual and strange pattern of its plan. Choirs of angels, trained and organized, give forth strange music; and the blending of many harmonies sends forth a symphony of sound that stirs the hearer to the very depths of being. Beautiful and rare is the outcome of this strange adventure in planetary life, and many and marvelous are the Beings who have shared in the achievement.

Great Watcher Approves Planet.—Long ages ago, after eons of effort and struggle to form a vehicle which could be used for man's habitation upon this planet, the Solar Lords so far succeeded in their task as to win the approval of the Great Watcher. It will be remembered that the world was created amid the shouts of laughter of the Gods. This might well be, for it was no small feat to obtain a physical body which could meet the needs of functioning on the planet, and yet bear some semblance of divine man, which it must ultimately duplicate. In the end, a fair measure of success was gained, and the Great Watcher gave approval, and himself took over the task of completing the undertaking and of leading man out of the abyss into which he had fallen.

THE COURTS OF HEAVEN

Angelic Hosts.—In the Courts of Heaven are choirs of the Angelic Hosts who bear witness to their origin in paeans of praise to their Solar Lord, each group to his own. For to this strange, sad ruin have come volunteer souls not only for incarnation as humans, but also to share in the Heavenly Hosts and increase their power and purpose. These heavenly volunteers were required to have passed through human evolution, however, before coming here and to have reached a stage of high superhuman development—for the risks they ran by associating themselves with this doomed world were great—lest they fail and do more harm than good. Therefore, an understanding of human evolution was a requisite.

Bands of Associates.—These great Solar Lords came with bands of their associates and retainers at various periods of the earth's history, and took over certain departments of the inner work for long periods of time, successively.

Some later associated themselves more closely with human evolution, and entered upon human incarnation. This entailed dangerous sacrifices and involved them in the race Karma. Sometimes the suffering was hideous, as these Rulers of celestial force tried to adjust themselves to human vehicles. Often the force they carried became misdirected and destructive through the limited and imperfect vision of the human mind.

Those who followed the purely religious and artistic line and lived in a world apart, as it were, misdirected their efforts least. Those, however, who definitely entered upon the rulership of man and the guidance of human affairs came to strange disaster. Yet, through it all, they poured into human mass consciousness new lines of force and distributed celestial energies into the fermenting pool of human corruption.

Courts of Heaven.—Bearing these concepts in mind, one may turn again to the study of the inner worlds—the Courts of Heaven. Here, indeed, greater success accompanied the efforts of the volunteers. Here, the great heavenly Choristers found a field for their influence, and so the Messengers of God, remembering somewhat of the inner glory, might well say—

Our Father which art in Heaven,
Thy will be done on *earth*,
As it is done in Heaven (the higher
level of the mental plane).

Here, the great bands of volunteer Devas gathered at appointed times and made about this dim earth a shining garden of delight. Little by little, reflections of the splendour built there became reflected down through the denser envelopes like mirages in a desert, of fertile oases and mighty cities. The tradition of glory became embodied in the ideals of Paradise. Nay, further, subordinate groups of Devas sought to build with the aid of devout human spirits in the lesser inner worlds replicas of some of the glories they had glimpsed and to some degree they succeeded. Hence, the Valhallas of ancient myth and legend.

Refuges.—Into these lesser Paradises, built by the lesser Devas, were admitted only the worthy humans as they passed out of incarnation. But the tradition of these refuges, and the great joy to be experienced in their attainment, permeated at last the envelope of the earth and roused humans to sacrifice earthly pleasures for glories of the inner worlds.

So, slowly, the tradition of beauty, of joy in the inner worlds seeped into human consciousness, and the glories brought by volunteer Solar Lords, and established about this benighted planet, began to shed their influence direct upon the lost race.

The Courts of Heaven are royal affairs at which the Solar Lords have each their appointed place and office. Some dim likeness of this original splendour has drifted down to earth in the splendour of monarchs and their royal state.

The central ruling figure of the Heavenly Court changes from time to time, as the office is held successively by Lords of a certain rank. A replica of this is seen in Masonry. Only those who have proved their wisdom, capacity and devotion are permitted to attend the great courts, and through the ages, the Master of the Court changes. This depends not upon choice, but upon the precession of the Equinoxes. As a new Star and Solar Group becomes dominant, the highest representative of the Group enters upon His duties, and becomes Overlord of the Planet, replacing that Lost Lord of our world who atones elsewhere, with dire struggles, for his disastrous failure.

Star Angels.—In the reign of these Overlords is the secret of the Star Angels, and the reason why it is stated that only those belonging to the same Star Angel know real unity. This must be so. For during the rule of one Star Angel, representing the power of one of the great Astrological houses, messengers are sent forth as saviours or prophets, to sound the note of that Star in the planet, and to rouse to response as many humans as possible who shall, if their efforts are determined enough, in the end join the court of that Star Angel and return with Him at last to His dominion, as part of His retinue. So shall humanity be gradually drawn away from this planet; with each dispensation a certain number achieve and become enrolled as members of that staff. "I and my Father are one." So indeed it is, for the Messenger is the beloved Son of the Father, sent out to summon the hosts of men to enroll in His ranks. "The way to the Father is through Me"—so indeed must it be— through the Messenger of the Star Angel.

Lesser Prophets.—Not only are these Messengers sent out by the Star Angels for the purpose of attaching souls to the Supreme Staff of Heaven, but there are lesser prophets sent out from the lesser Paradises, to rouse those humans who can grasp only a part of the truth. If they can attain the lesser Paradises, they can see at times something of the greater glory, and return to earth better prepared to answer to the note of the Supreme Ruler for the period. Mohammed was one of these lesser messengers, also Swedenborg and others.

The Central Star.—In the Courts of Heaven, each group coming from one great Solar group during the ceremonies invokes the power and blessing of its central Star. Yet the ceremonies are dominated always by the group whose Star is in the ascendant at that time. This one group, as it were, becomes the leader of the great Choir during the ascendancy of the Star to whom it owes allegiance.

Seers and Prophets.—In the Courts of Heaven are many Lords, with their retinues. These send their subordinates into incarnation to carry the note that each Lord has come to sound into the world of men. Some come as seers and prophets; some as artists and musicians; some as builders and organizers. But they stand out from those about them as individuals unique and remote, touched by a divine fire, as indeed they are, for they are flooded by the power of the Lord who sent them.

Lords of the Starry Spaces.—These great Lords, however, look to an Overlord who now has taken charge of evolution. It is hoped to raise humanity to the point where some of its own people can govern the planet, and release from long and arduous duty these Lords of the Starry Spaces, sojourners these many ages far from their own dwelling places.

The Laws of Evolution.—The old idea of a limited Heaven will in time give place to an understanding of the laws of evolution, and the methods whereby men can achieve most readily the conquest of themselves and of the material world, for this determines the length of their imprisonment. If plans can be carried out as now visioned, one by one the Great Solar Lords will depart, carrying with them in their train those who have learned to follow them and to respond fully to their dominant note. There are Devas being trained now, belonging to this evolution, or permanently associated with it, who will replace the retinues of some of the Star Lords in their duties. Similarly, there are humans being trained to relieve the Star Lords of their burdens, and to undertake the governance of the inner and outer forces of the planet.

Work of the Devas.—The work of the Devas is to draw to the planet certain solar and inter-planetary forces for storage in great reservoirs and for distribution to the kingdoms of nature and, under special conditions, to the kingdom of man. Likewise, they keep playing about the planet in great belts of magnetic current on all planes, certain forces necessary to evolution. These forces are foreign to the planet, and do not belong here naturally, but have been kept here artificially to foster growth, ever since man was cast upon the surface of the cinder, and the planet had to be made habitable to him.

The Great Mother.—It is of interest to realize that but for the intervention of certain compassionate Beings—of these the principal one being the Great Mother of Waters, Our Lady of Venus—man's destiny would have been far different. When his Leader fell, he would, unless rescued, have lost his opportunity to evolve and sunk back into the realms of demons, to evolve once more from the earliest beginnings—a long road. But compassionate Great Ones intervened. Here one has something of the concept of original sin and the salvation by sacrifice. And much is true of this ancient teaching. However, man was not saved: he could not be lifted from the pit into which he had fallen. But it was made possible for him to attain salvation by his own efforts, assisted by the helping hands of the Great Solar Lords. It is analogous to what happens in shipwreck. When rescue boats are sent out to save the survivors of a disaster, the rescue of any individual depends upon his willingness to accept the aid of the rescuers. Else he will sink. So, in human evolution, some men are sinking into the pit of demons, because they refuse to avail themselves of the aid vouchsafed.

The limitations of the more orthodox religions are due to the effort to fit them to men's minds. The average man cannot benefit from a religion which is too tolerant. It lacks intensive power to draw him away from material pleasures which debase him.

The work of the chosen leaders of men is to control and to administer on all planes the forces generated by man and to relate this work to that of the Devas.

The echoing timbre of the stars chimes through the vaults of space like the music of singing choirs in the vaulted nave of a cathedral. The tissue of the stars is fiery vapor condensed by the cool waters of the atmosphere with which each is surrounded.

Receptions Held.—Each star is a great exalted and mysterious Personage with attendant planets holding court for the worship and adoration by the lesser beings. So does the Court of Heaven hold reception for those of greater circles and cycles; and there gather to its throne great Lords and Mighty Powers radiant in splendour and display.

This Court of Heaven is held from period to period for the renewing of authority and understanding in the lesser ones. To it are summoned High Lords and lesser Lords from the far corners of the Systems to pay homage to the Overlord and to receive in turn honours and recognition according to each one's rank and deserts.

One of these great Courts has been or is now being held in Sirius and our Kumara attended by his Council, has received his summons and fared forth upon the open road —opened for this purpose by Higher Powers, and safeguarded by choirs of Devas who by their song send sweeping rhythms through space upon which lesser Lords may travel. So surrounded by his Planetary guard, and escorted by the Singing Angels, our great Lord fared forth upon the open way. There he was received with due honour and ranked among his peers. His attendants grouped about him and lent him glory for the honour of the planet, each displaying to the full honours and powers acquired upon this planet or in earlier manvantaras or gained through intensive effort in the Systems open for special aspirants to cosmic honours.

Bestowing of Honour.—A great ceremony was enacted wherein those who had served the Systems in some special capacity and with some signal success were given rank and honour by the Overlord. Although Sirius was the stage for the great court, many higher Lords from Higher Systems attended. However, the actual bestowing of honour was done by the Overlord of Sirius, because it was those in this System who were thus being honoured.

One received high honours and new rank—that of Supervisory Overlord of Systems of the tenth degree, with the power to appoint his assistants. This involves almost constant travel from System to System, and the receiving of reports from all conditions in each rank. In clearer words, he is to receive the reports of the Overlords of each System below the tenth, and give counsel and advice to them as to the condition of their districts to the third Degree. There are others smaller and less evolved than we.

Another was given rank for power and endurance along the line of fiery pain, which opens new avenues upon the Golden Ways and gives authority of convoy and power of entrance into some councils upon Sirius. He has become an authority upon the use and distribution of certain fiery forces.

THE FIRES OF THE SPHERES

The fires of the spheres leave a trail across the heavens as they wheel and flash and turn again in their orbits. It is all a path of beauty seen with the cosmic eye.

Highways Between Sister Systems.—The trail of fire links planet to planet, and it is upon this trail that the avenues between the sister planets and between the sister Systems are opened. It is not possible to soar into endless space. There are Systems which we cannot touch nor enter since they are not related to us except in the most remote and distant way. But between sister Systems there are highways, traversed and traversible by the great officials of the Suns, who visit occasionally even the remote portions of their kingdoms.

When any important event or crisis nears upon a planet, the attention of many Solar Lords is drawn to it and they come here for observation and study. Sometimes they graciously stage a ceremonial for the purpose of diverting some of their royal power for the benefit of the planet they visit.

On such occasions, all the Lords of the Planetary Hierarchy gather, and often representatives from the Hierarchy of every planet in our small Solar System are summoned to attend. Great ceremonies ensue, which are shared by all the leading souls of a planet.

Strange Laws.—Our system is very vast, as are all Systems except those in the earliest stages of formation, of which we have small knowledge. Beginning with the small Solar Systems around a central Sun—and the small Suns around the greater Sun, it goes onward into great wheels and vortices beyond imagination. Seasons in these great Systems vary and there are periods when the highways are open—due to some magnetic polarity, which is governed by something far remote from us. Then visitors abound, and travel is encouraged. There are other great periods where the highways are dark and only specially prepared Solar Leaders venture far afield. Here again are strange laws coming from far-distant realms. These strange laws are the only sign we have of some remote and awful Intelligence which guides and governs the wheeling Systems.

THE TRAIL OF THE GOLDEN WAYS

To Whom It Is Open.—The trail of the Golden Ways lies open only to those who belong to the intercosmic Systems, and who won the right by power and by knowledge to travel from System to System.

The open road of the Cosmic Way is open to a few only in each System. Even among the Higher Lords, all have not the power to travel. There are many who cannot make the necessary atomic and magnetic adjustment to the varying atmospheres, just as many cannot endure the pressure of deep sea diving. It requires peculiar qualities and capacities. The trail of the Golden Ways is the highroad of the Systems, and links sister Systems and Universes. In the beginning, those who desire to follow this trail experiment only in a minor way with short journeys until their powers increase. Volunteers may come to a planet who are not Lords of the Open Way. In such cases they are brought by others and encased in a protective sheath until they reach the planet, and there adjust themselves to its peculiar atmosphere and necessities.

The Great Adventurers.—The Lords of the Golden Ways are the great adventurers and explorers of the Solar System, and just as explorers here bring back scientific data of their journeys, so the Golden Lords, as they are called, bring back reports of their investigations for scientific analysis and study. Often they take replicas of the planet or special phases of its development for the great central museums in the central Suns. Not only has each planet a record of its own history, but each central Sun has a record, condensed, of the many planets and Systems which circle about it. When the time for a new System arrives, the Logos-to-be studies long and earnestly the various methods of evolution, their advantages and their disadvantages.

Speed of Earth Evolution.—One thing may be said in favor of earth evolution. Its speed is remarkable and an enormous amount of experience, mental, emotional and physical, is condensed into a comparatively brief period. Moreover, it includes ultimate control over forces and regions of a low order which few evolutions contact and yet covers lofty achievements in high realms. Like the story of the Sinful Deva who chose to be a Rakshasa because he completed his doom so much more rapidly, so here those who evolve upon this rebellious planet complete their allotted tasks with great speed. The obedient evolutions mature easily but with great deliberation, and gain individual strength at a late period. Here the method of evolution is analogous to throwing a man overboard to teach him to swim. He swims or sinks. In life, he is cast upon a turbulent planet to find his own way with man and nature, both against him. He sinks or swims, and either way learns much. He has many forces to combat, and like a man in a maelstrom, succeeds in achieving peaceful waters only by supreme and heroic efforts. That demand upon his endurance, his will, and his intelligence matures him rapidly. It is not surprising, however, that long and woeful is the lamentation of humanity for its arduous and terrible lot.

Covers the Whole Milky Way.—The trail of the Golden Ways covers the whole of the Milky Way and our saucer-shaped Universe. It does not, as far as is known, go beyond the Universes included therein. Indeed, many of those who travel thereon travel only brief journeys. Even that is a notable accomplishment, confined to a few adventurous and specially prepared souls on each planet. Sometimes, however, convoys of visitors from neighboring planets are brought by the Golden Lords. In these cases, special safeguards are arranged and advantage taken of occasional magnetic conditions which permit of easier travel.

Latterly this planet has had many visitors. Interchange between planets of one solar System is not difficult, as the magnetic conditions are similar. It is the passing beyond the "ring-pass-not" of a System that is dangerous. This requires a great adaptability, flexibility and endurance of the atomic structure. There must be possible a great variety of tensions, a gamut of intensity and condensation suited to the varying atmospheres. It means the power to key up and key down the atomic vibrations, without undue strain. Part of this versatility comes both through the endurance of pain and the power of expansion of the vehicles. Great expansion of the vehicles brings terrific strain on the atoms, but it is necessary to enable one to pass into far more rarefied atmospheres. Otherwise, the higher vehicles under the more rarefied conditions might cease to cohere and function. Pain on the other hand gives intensity and rapidity and endurance to the atoms. It tempers, purifies and toughens them. Remember this in hours of pain or strain.

THE GREAT CONNECTING AVENUES

Correspond to Nervous System.—In the spirals of space there are winding passages which lead directly from one

System to another, and which correspond to the nervous System of the human body, whereby impacts upon one portion of the body have their repercussion through the entire organism. For each great nebular group, there is a nebular heart and brain, the heart controlling the currents which feed the great Solar Systems with their myriad dependent earths, and the brain carrying and controlling the electric energy of the System and interweaving the units so that they respond as a whole to the will and intentions of the Master Mind behind it all.

In other words, the heart centre is magnetic; the mind centre, electric. Blood carries magnetism. You will notice that full-blooded persons are magnetic and usually strongly sexed. Mental types are more electric, less full-blooded, less sexed, but capable of stirring men's minds and firing their enthusiasms. One of the magnetic type may be a great orator and leader of men, but his following will be personal, because he stirs their emotions. The electric type disseminates ideas with dynamic power in them which sets men's minds to thinking and lays the foundation for all great reform movements of a political or social nature. In one case, people follow because they love. In the other, they follow because they think. Certain great leaders combine somewhat of both, but one force is usually dominant.

Unity of Body of Planets.—As one develops in evolution, one can learn to contact these great connecting avenues and enter more fully into the life forces of the universe. The significance of the science of Astrology stems from the unity of the great body of planets; but as yet the extra-solar forces are not sufficiently understood to account for the influences they wield. The Precession of the Equinoxes has a greater influence upon the action of the planetary forces at any given time than humans now grasp. The direct influence of the dominant Equinox upon the sun is of paramount importance, since it changes in the System the force of every planet and modifies, intensifies and changes its native influences.

The keynote of the Equinox dominates the age. The planetary influences are merely minor and subordinate chords within the major harmony.

CYCLES OF THE SOLAR SYSTEM

Its Cosmic Pulse.—The fires in the central Sun wax and wane, as magnetic currents sweep through the Universe. There is a periodic heating and cooling, expansion and contraction, similar to breathing and the circulation of the blood. This Cosmic pulse shows itself in sun conditions, sun spots, and the periods of heat and cold upon the planets. There are several cycles: the daily pulse, the yearly pulse and the climacteric pulse, extending over great periods of time.

We are at the present time entering into a great climacteric which will increase the heat and, therefore, the activity of our System. Lesser cycles are often based upon greater ones, so that planet cycles coincide with Solar and Cosmic cycles. The present cycle affects not only the planet, the Solar System, the Sirian System, but circles far beyond, and opportunity is being seized to swing this planet into new channels with the help of forces now loosed. This was foreseen and great efforts turned to preparing the way, as one takes advantage of a larger wave to ride farther in upon the beach.

Its Speed of Progress.—The actual speed of progress of our Solar System depends upon how fast this earth, the most material and backward planet, can be forced forward. No System can move faster than its weakest link. Similarly, the Sirian System is held back to the speed of our Solar System, and so on, through countless circles.

Therefore, upon the fate of this insignificant planet hang larger or heavier consequences. Hence, the efforts of great volunteer Lords to assist its evolution.

III · HUMAN EVOLUTION

III · HUMAN EVOLUTION

COURSE OF THE CYCLES IN EVOLUTION

The course of the cycles in evolution has been long a subject of study. It must be remembered, however, that human evolution is not normal, and has not followed the even progress of cycles habitual to most evolutionary stages. At a critical point, it fell out of line and descended into a world in which it was not intended to dwell, and therefore into cycles of evolution quite foreign to it.

The Animal Kingdom.—After all, one must remember that the larger animal life here exists only because man fell into generation or physical vehicles. The animal kingdom, subordinate to man and wholly dependent upon him, followed him into the material world to provide vehicles for young in-coming souls to contact man and thus to prepare them for humanity. Here, too, the errors became manifest.

Animals as well as men took on some of the characteristics of the demon evolution, into whose department they had fallen, and who are the real heritors of the planet. Animals, some of them, began to have terrible attributes of savagery, but especially those brought into contact with man and trained by him for his own cruel purposes of destruction.

Let us interpolate here a point of significance. Man copied the rebellion of his Lord, and set his *mind* in opposition to that of the Solar Logos, and disobeyed through mind (Serpent).

65

Man's Rebellion.—After eating of the Tree of Knowledge, he fell into generation and entered physical bodies, with their inherent sex naturés. This was a result and not a cause of the disobedience, and was the only safeguard at his then stage of development. It forced him into the state of subordination to passion and pain, lest he commit the fatal sin of eating of the tree of life before he had completed his cycle of evolution. This would have spelt disaster in every sense, for the whole human effort would have been wasted. He would have caused a short circuit and returned to his original condition without having gained the powers resulting from the cycle of evolution intended for him. By his rebellion, he has greatly delayed his progress and entered intolerable hardships. But having seized knowledge—or literally asserted the powers of mind before their time—he must be forced under the humiliation and yoke of physical weakness, pain and passion to prevent greater disaster.

The Karmic Burden.—Adam and Eve are symbols of the first humanity which shared in the disobedience of their Overlord; and all humanity since then, as they take upon themselves bodies from that source, take, too, the Karmic burden of their forebears.

Man should have developed obedience first, then wisdom and finally will. He reversed these, and only by obedience and submission can now escape the toils into which he has fallen. Certain types of animals belong to the planet—insects, fish, some birds, reptiles and rodents. They obey a different law and are menacing to humans. Those other greater beasts who menace humans do so only because of man's own evil training—wolves, tigers, leopards, lions.

The serpent is the symbol of the mind, because at a low

stage it is dangerous and deadly, and only when translated to higher regions shows forth its other side of wisdom and magic. Magic is deadly to all in its early stages, when man has not developed wisdom and love.

The Silent Watcher of the Planetary System

Human and Demon.—Now it is well to consider the method of evolution on this planet. In all religions the duality has been emphasized that men might know and recognize their danger from association with the destructive forces of nature. These demonic beings have inhabited the planet for untold periods. Ultimately they will be used as a leaven to overcome inertia in very slow moving humanities who evolve through interminable periods and require energizing. Their destructive power curbed, their wrath and malice burnt low, they can be distributed with beneficial effect upon these slumbrous planets, to mix and blend with the beneficent elements already well established and therefore safe from overbalance.

Mixing of the Two Evolutions.—Unfortunately, on this planet a human evolution is evolving of a highly unstable nature, fiery, unbalanced and explosive. The admixture of the destructive forces here is much to be deprecated. They over-accentuate a condition already dangerous, and every effort is being made to prevent the mixing of the two evolutions.

The Fall of Humanity.—A great part of our present humanity came from another evolution, which proved too unstable in temperament to be used in the way first intended, and they were sent to the densest planet to temper and strengthen their cohesive power. They were intended to

live only in the atmosphere of the planet, and never to contact either the surface or the inner chambers of our earth.
But owing to the error already discussed, they were driven
from Eden and precipitated onto the earth's surface. Here
their lot became a hard one, and it was rendered even
harder by the disobedient mortals who contacted the demon
evolution and sought to use its powers selfishly. Then indeed
did suffering result. Pandora's box was an allegory of far-
reaching truth.

Racial Evolution Hastened.—For thousands of years the
demonic power was unchecked. The cycle of their greatest
power from the evolutionary point of view, owing to the
specific density of matter in the planet, coincided with the
period of man's greatest period of sensibility to material
emanations—his nadir from spiritual light. This danger was
foreseen long in advance, and all possible precautions taken.
It was then that volunteers arrived for special service, and
the decision made to hasten the racial evolution at the cost
of untold suffering, and likewise of intolerable effort.

Era of Danger Past.—The Silent Watcher of the Planetary System entered the field and undertook the personal
supervision of this planet at its more critical era, having
watched and directed the development of the successive
Chains to this point. More and more he has associated himself with the evolution of our humanity until, through super-
human efforts, the era of danger has passed and man is
emerging into safety and redemption. Just what this has
involved is difficult to explain. Little by little more will be
made clear. But bear this in mind, many of the chosen
assistants fell under the domination of the destructive forces,
made ghastly Karmic debts, and emerged with powers re-

duced and much for which to account. In time all these will redeem themselves, adjust their debts and turn at last the full play of their saving energies to the planet. In the meantime, however, greatly increased responsibilities and burdens have been added to that lofty Being who had involved himself in this melancholy debacle.

SPIRITUAL GIANTS

A Day of Judgment.—The Great Lords who have come to aid this planet carry a new and different power from anything as yet known here. They belong to a group of Systems so lofty, so tender and so beautiful that pain and anguish are scarcely known, even by hearsay. They are come to pour love and compassion in such high measure upon this anguished world that they will lift it beyond the reach of the demonic hosts.

This cannot come all at once. It must of necessity be a gradual process, dependent to some extent upon the actual physical re-organization of the planet so that it may be ordered, cleansed, purified and divested of those souls who cannot accept the new dispensation. It is indeed a Day of Judgment; and those who cannot respond to love and to compassion must be set aside for the protection of the rest.

Karmic Heredity.—There is a Karmic heredity which must be cleansed, and those strains in humanity which have partaken of the demonic atoms and which are, therefore, open to response from demonic stimuli, must be prevented from creating. The sterilizing of criminals will gradually accomplish this, and the noble strains of humanity will populate the earth.

It will be, in a sense, a condition similar to the Flood,

when the best of the race was salvaged to make a new people. Only in this case it will be done by science, not through the elemental powers. It is necessary to remember that this cleansing of the cup must be accomplished by men themselves. But it will be facilitated and hastened by the new force which will carry on those that respond to it so swiftly that they will tower in strength and purpose above their present stature, as if they had become giants, and so indeed they will have become—spiritual giants. Outstanding figures of the past who have now returned into incarnation will rise to spiritual splendours that will dazzle the people into obedience.

It is impossible for the new Lords to act directly upon the evil and dangerous forces in humanity. They cannot. It is not in their line of evolution. They must rely upon their human agents to do these things, and to prepare the way. Indeed, if a sufficient group of egos had not through countless ages been driven forward in intelligence, sacrifice and power, so that they could be counted on to take hold of the governance and policing of the world, this great day of salvation had not dawned.

THE STARS IN THEIR COURSES

Superiors and Inferiors.—The stars in their courses revolve about greater principals in ever greater orbits. So is built the vast system of which we are a part. It is the law that the greater shall have the lesser revolve about them, and the lesser in turn shall have revolve about them those even smaller than themselves. Thus is order established. It is a fundamental principle of human consciousness to seek to find those greater than oneself about whom one can revolve. One finds this pivotal point in various ways. In boyhood and early stages of civilization physical contest marks one superior in combat. In later times mental ability marks the leader. At last it comes through spiritual achievement. Yet the principle remains the same—allegiance and service to those whom we recognize as superior. It has been the basis of marriage, wherein the woman followed her mate who proved himself stronger in certain dominant traits. Where a man failed to dominate, the woman sought elsewhere until she found her superior, and the weaker man in turn found peace with an even weaker woman.

There are some exceptions to this rule—those who resent domination and take issue with the law of obedience to superior strength. These be the rebels, and because they have not obedience, they stand as lone units against an organized world. They seek obedience, but refuse to render it. And only as one renders it above may one exact it from below. Otherwise, tyranny results.

VOLUNTEER SOULS

The Good Followers.—There is yet another phase of human evolution to discuss. When the volunteer souls came to give assistance to the Great Being, there came also less experienced but gentle souls to share in the modifying of turmoil here. These souls could not alone meet the problems of existence upon this planet, their natures were too timid, gentle, non-resisting and inactive. The positive power which can alone force the nature of man to rise and to conquer danger, obstacles, disaster, and which alone could carry man forward to conquest, dwelt not in them. But they could make good followers, useful material, obedient and pliable when courageously led—the sheep and the goats.

Inheritance of the Meek.—"Blessed are the meek, for they shall inherit the earth." This will indeed be their reward when the battle is won and peace reigns. Then will these gentle souls come into their heritage of peace upon a tranquilized planet. The others who have borne the brunt of battle will not remain here, too passive a spot for their tumultuous energies, but will seek out new fields to conquer, new dangers to meet and to surmount. There are many places open to the warrior souls.

The three higher Hindu castes represent the three types of souls who have come to this planet. The priest and the warrior belong not here. Their rays do not normally function here. They have represented the inner worlds of power and of faith. The great Vaisha or merchant caste, which is peaceful and flourishes only in peace, represents the true residents of earth, and will carry on the civilization when the others have passed out, no longer needed in a peaceful world. They belong to the realm of form, these traders, and the rising of business as the guide and arbiter of life foretells the approaching hour, which shall see the dismissal of the others, the priest and the warrior. They will have for a time minor roles to play, but as soon as they reach the Arhat stage, they will depart to other realms.

THE LAW OF RETRIBUTION

The law of retribution is exact. It does indeed demand an eye for an eye, and the Mosaic Law was based upon occult fact, and was written into tablets to make clear something of the true law of evolution to a still ignorant people. At that period justice was a law man could understand; it was the limit of his spiritual growth. Later, in the time of the Buddha and of the Christ, came the newer teaching of love, sacrifice and forbearance. At first, only a few in incarnation were advanced enough to understand and accept the new teaching. Gradually the world is learning through slow ages the spiritual law of renunciation of revenge.

In business men begin to recognize that "thy neighbor is as thyself," and that the security and success of all depend upon the well-being of each. Soon the lesson will be learned among nations, and each will be permitted to exercise and develop his special genius, and thus contribute to the mutual good.

The Mysteries of Isis

The mysteries of Isis revealed more of occult truth than any others in the past ten thousand years. Egypt was to pass down to history as the great and beneficent civilization of that period, and to form a model for the unfolding of the new civilization at the beginning of the new age. Service, beauty, simplicity and grandeur, kindliness and peace were to be copied from it.

There are several ways of work—through fear, through interest, through love, through patriotism. Probably the safest is self-interest. This was the key of Egypt, and will be the key of the new world.

Self-Interest.—Self-interest sounds selfish. It means really awakening the individual to know that the welfare of the state brings peace and plenty to him and to his; that he shares in its progress and profits by its order. It makes every man a trustee for the public good. It promotes friendliness and provokes good will. Our great trusts are appealing to this motive, and it makes the most prosperous and contented form of government.

THE CONTROL OF ELEMENTAL FORCES

As men learn to control and invoke and direct certain great powers of the planet, they will learn to dissipate many human ills. Much of the suffering of humanity has come from exposure to unfriendly or unconcerned elemental forces, fire and cold, rain and drought. Gradually the increasing knowledge of man, dedicated to the service of humanity, will achieve the control of these physical elemental forces. Much progress has already been made, and the development of machinery assures the future physical well-being of the world.

In older days, many physical laws were controlled by inner powers of divine or spiritual origin. Now evolution has progressed where these things may be done by scientific and physical means, such as the control of gravity. This is wise, for it opens the knowledge to the masses and saves them from superstition, perhaps the deadliest foe to human welfare.

Disease.—In a similar way conquest of disease will be achieved. Spiritual healing has had its place, just as spiritual physics, but it will be better for man if he relies more and more upon himself, and less and less upon occult agencies, who often open him to obsession, or give him an improper idea of their importance. Man must escape from the domination of the lower gods. This only can he do as he finds within himself power over material conditions.

THE BLOOM OF HUMANITY

With the coming of new forces into this planet, the bloom of the flower of humanity will be much hastened. Up to this time has been witnessed only the preparation of the soil, the dark earth, the fertilization through blood and anguish, and always the deep burial of the bulb and root of spiritual things beneath the dark surface of human life. Yet now with the new sun forces, as in a greenhouse, soon the first green shafts of the plant itself appear, promise of the spiritual flower which is to come. The bloom itself will be upon the inner planes of spirit, in the finer bodies of humanity, but the root must draw its life and sustenance from the soil of earth, from the dense body of physical man.

Man's Kingdom.—Man's kingdom is indeed in the inner worlds, but it can be won only as he sends his roots deep into the soil of human life, grips it firmly and then reaches from that firm base upward to the spiritual sun, so that he shall at last burst forth in the full bloom of divine glory. That glory shall be the flowering of the soul, and the fragrance shall permeate and irradiate human life. For man will know the realities then of human incarnation. He will assay truly the place of physical life, but he will centre his consciousness in the realms of the spirit where blooms the flower of the soul, and he will find there the peace and glory whose promise led him ever on to renewed efforts to break the thrall of earth while it bound him close. The analogy is so clear. It has been often used, but perhaps not truly understood. The flower blooms in the inner worlds, but sends back the consciousness of liberation, glory, perfume and beauty along its stem to the tentacles below ground—

firmly rooted in the dark soil, the matrix of the celestial bloom.

The Awakened Spirit.—Do not despise earth, neither the dark soil nor the evil-smelling manure which nourishes the roots. From this crude base springs all the glory of celestial beauty, and without it the bloom of the soul of man were impossible. But the time of seed and sorrow is past. Spring is here, and the new forces of the spiritual sun intensified by and concentrated by the clear glass of the hot-house shall soon bring the plant to growth. The simile is correct. For the great Beings who have vouchsafed help to this planet act as foci of spiritual force and concentrate and intensify the powers of the spiritual sun, like glass, for the benefit of humanity. Under this new protection and out-pouring, humanity will come rapidly to maturity, and the pain and effort of growth, of imprisonment, of evil and of pain, which are manifestations of the pressure of matter, will be forgotten in the glory of the awakened spirit.

It is but natural that those seeds which have already made the greatest effort, which have already advanced furthest toward spiritual bloom and spiritual potency, should profit most and soonest. These will shoot upward to adeptship and to spiritual mastery with amazing speed, especially when these forces are finally focused upon the physical plane through agencies in physical bodies. In the blaze of new power and light, the particles of earth which have clung to the tender shoots which marked the earliest promise of spiritual things will be swept away, and soul after soul will rise in its glory like an awakened god, new risen in the dawn.

Man's Liberation.—As man, in years to come, learns to see and to hear upon all three planes of the personality, his sense of limitation and frustration will cease. No longer will he be buried in matter, struggling blindly to force upward to the light. He will dwell in the light and, as he enters upon his spiritual labours, forget the pain and pressure of the darkness which lies about his feet, and gives them a firm base upon which to stand.

REIGN OF PEACE

The pain here is due to the original curse when Adam and Eve were driven from Paradise. And the reason for the intensive anguish of this planet is due to the doom pronounced and to the efforts to complete it and to escape. The leaders labour incessantly to help the race, and pay huge penalties in pain for their sacrifices.

In the early days of a planet, even of this chain, harmony rules, for men are still docile to authority. But as evolution unfolds their natures, the rebellious and demonic strains begin to manifest more and more fully. In other planets animals do not prey upon each other as here. They gather their sustenance from materials provided for their use, and the group Deva controls the number born. You see harmlessness in some of our own animals, as in rabbits and deer. But here where the manifestation of the original life of the planet brings into being pests which batten upon plant, animal and man, the same forces cause animals to batten upon men, and men on animals.

The reign of peace in its fullness can only come as gradually some of these things are controlled, and man turns away from living sacrifices to the serving of life by science. But these things can be brought about only little by little.

In your lives get as much of joy as possible, of that original joy which was intended for all the Sons of God; the joy of the bird on the wing, the joy of the gazelle as it snuffs the dawn; the joy of the wave as it sweeps before the wind.

Cultivate this joy of living which is the true expression of God's purpose. Education should be a joy, and will become so, as years pass.

IV · DEMONIC EVOLUTION

1. DEMONS OF THE DARK FACE AND THE FIERY DEMONS
   Earth-born
   Original Inhabitants

2. FIERY DEMONS
   Magic
   Will and Magnetism

3. WATERY DEMONS
   Storm Winds
   Fog and Icebergs
   Atlantean Monsters
   Destroying Flames
   Mountain Magnetism
   Adepts
   Chelas

4. EONIC DAMNATION
   Spirit of the Earth
   Mixing of Evolutions
   Semi-human Entities
   Imprisoned Souls
   Hells

5. DEMONIC FORCES AND BATTLING HOSTS
   Invasions of Disease
   Cleansing of Evil Areas

6. HATRED HAS ITS PURPOSE

IV · DEMONIC EVOLUTION

DEMONS OF THE DARK FACE AND THE FIERY DEMONS

Earth-born.—The demons of the dark face and the demons of the fiery face both exist. Demons of the dark face fear light and are night-born offspring of evil magnetism and of the evil things which creep and crawl when the sun vanishes. They are easily controlled by fire which cleanses and purifies. Think of these as like the slimy creeping things that dwell in mud and ooze. They are earth-born and belong to the surface of our planet, progeny of man's own low evolution and evil desires and corruption.

Original Inhabitants.—The demons of the fiery face are the original inhabitants of the planet, clean spawn of fire, in their pristine state unevolved and destructive. They have been liberated from the inner chambers of the cinder by natural phenomena and by man's curiosity and intervention. There are things which are not lawful. The ancient curse of rebellion still flourishes in modern man, a desire to investigate the unlawful. Unlawful not because evil, but because dangerous. It is unscientific to refuse to obey law, in universes, in planets, in laboratories, in machinery. Man has the right to challenge tradition but not to desire the unlawful because forbidden. That is folly. Let him understand the reason but not challenge fate by stupid disobedience. In all departments of life certain methods, things, combinations menace the entire race: a miner smoking where fire damp lurks; a machinist refusing to observe caution; a locomotive engineer who drinks. But men learn slowly. And to safeguard the race, many things were decreed as unlawful by religious custom.

FIERY DEMONS

Magic.—The clear light of the sun acts as a cleanser to all evil of a certain type, but this evil is mostly man-made or connected in some way with man's emanations. That is why evil magic must be performed by man in the night. Most of this magic is moon magic and has to do with man's body, its secretions, sensations and emanations. It is the product of watery influences. But the fiery demons have no fear of sunlight and thrive best where heat and light are most intense. They are often controlled and affected by water. Legends of the past speak of beings unable to pass over a body of water, and exorcised by holy water, etc. Each element has its own mysteries. Much can be understood if one learns to segregate the expressions of evil into their elements, for their expression will conform to the element which governs them and will be controlled by its opposing element. Those things which belong to the surface of the earth, to water and to the moon, to growing things and physical forms are controlled and cleansed by fire and the will. But the fiery demons who come from the centre chambers of the earth direct are controlled by water and personal magnetism.

Will and Magnetism.—There is perhaps a question how to differentiate between will and magnetism, but there is a real distinction. Will is a fiery flame, an electrical power, which bores and burns. Magnetism is a controlling power, similar to hypnotism and mesmerism. It paralyzes and congeals. One is connected with the earth. Demons from the fiery core of the earth, having had no contact with human bodies, are not concerned with noisome black magic such as Voodooism and the like. They are rather the flaming destruction which fires the mind to madness, illustrated in mob violence, fanaticism, destroying wrath.

In general, man follows the line of will, women the line of magnetism, though these are often reversed in individual cases. Magnetism is akin to water, making things grow and increase. It is soothing, binding and loving. Fire is nearer to will in its pure essence, less balanced, less controlled, more unstable and more dangerous.

All great leaders have personal magnetism to a large degree. It is connected with a full sex nature and has much governing power.

WATERY DEMONS

Storm Winds.—Over the open seas hover demons who have been oceanbound. There are those likewise who are landbound. These cannot cross water. So there are those waterbound who harry the sailor folk and the innocent vessels which contact their abodes. It is only at certain periods that their fury can vent itself, certain magnetic and electric conditions which liberate their destructive energies and permit their play. Then come the great storms out of the North and out of the East. Certain winds liberate these energies so they are called storm winds. But in truth it is not the winds which liberate the storm, but these malignant forces riding the winds and liberated by them, which hurl the etheric into confusion and disturb climatic conditions.

Fog and Icebergs.—Sometimes there are malignant entities who inhabit certain regions and seek to destroy men and ships. Such a region is the Grand Banks of Newfoundland, where the fog prevails and icebergs lurk. Here the conditions are not due to the demons, but to certain natural currents and flows; yet advantage is taken of these conditions by the demons, and their residence, as it were, established there, just as a great cuttlefish might lurk in some natural cavern or crevasse under the surface of the ocean.

Ancient mariners were more right than men now know in their ideas of evil spirits and monsters of the deep, ready to seize the unwary. Being psychic—the simple peasant mind is instinctive like a dog's—they sensed these things. Actually, entire distrust in superstition is an enormous preventive to psychic disturbances, for it hardens the mind to unwelcome intrusions and protects the vehicles from response to fear. Therefore, the present materialistic age was essential in order to close the lower vehicles before the higher were sensitized. There is danger even now in the sensitizing of the lower vehicles, and should be avoided. A certain hardening of the mind will repel psychic invasions.

Meanwhile, much power is being taken from the unruly elementals and mankind is actually in less danger than formerly. New difficulties, however, will arise and more elementals will seize control of humans than before, as in the process of destroying the centres of evil magnetism on the planet they are being torn from their lairs. Hence there will be less security among humans, more distrust of each other. More care must be exercised to protect innocent humans from the assault of obsessed or semi-obsessed beings.

Atlantean Monsters.—In the deep caverns of the sea are curious monsters that science has not yet uncovered. They will, when found, teach something of the early life on the planet. But also there are evil entities who have taken refuge there in the Atlantean days, relics of the ancient Atlantean evil, who remained beneath the waters in etheric form when the lands sank. And there they weave their evil spells and do damage to thousands of good ships and innocent people. In part, they are the causes of the West Indies hurricanes, and these cannot be controlled until they have been routed out.

Destroying Flames.—But here lies a potent difficulty. For effective work in destroying elementals, one needs to use force drawn from the physical body—physical matter to act as the basis of the sealing envelope from which they cannot escape, and into which then the destroying flames —electric currents—are shot. And no one can get near enough to them physically to make available force from their own physical bodies. So the problem remains as yet unsolved, and the storms continue. In time probably a solution can be found, but at present the plans of the Hierarchy on that line are halted.

Less difficult is the problem of the desert forces. These can be overcome by water, a most potent agent. And, as the earth blooms under the new plans for dams and irrigation, much of their virulence can be overcome. In time the cauldrons beneath the surface of the earth, whence they come, can be sealed above and their modes of egress closed. But the sea folk leave us still with an arduous problem.

Mountain Magnetism.—In the high mountains, not actively volcanic, there exists a purity of atmosphere found nowhere else. Not only are the evil hosts of air and sea unable to function there, but their offspring, the destructive germs, likewise cannot persist there. In time this will be recognized, and hospitals for the sick and the insane will be established at very high altitudes. It is probable that lesser criminals also would benefit from such conditions. There is something about the isolation and solemnity of high mountains that awakens the slumbering soul.

It is for this reason that the adepts who practice phenomena dwell in these lofty and remote solitudes. There, with less danger, they can train their chelas and sensitize them. The Masters who dwell in the world must wear a protective sheath and cannot open themselves too greatly to occult forces, because of the destructive emanations in which they live. Therefore, their methods and training, their work, plans and purposes, are quite different from those remote ones who as yet labour for continents and races, not peoples and persons individually.

Adepts.—This does not mean that adepts in touch with humanity are totally blind to the finer forces. They look deep into the workings of the human heart, and guide the plans of the Hierarchy from a practical basis. They see and grasp the plan for the nations, and work with it from their own position. It is highly important to differentiate between the two schools, and to recognize the place of each, and the value of each method of training disciples.

Chelas.—The chelas of the second school rarely know their Master, but carry out his plans along intellectual and inspirational lines, as the great scientists, organizers and statesmen have done through the ages. Their very independence of judgment and action safeguard them in the troubled conditions in which they work. One can know them by their genius, their altruism, and their capacity for leadership.

EONIC DAMNATION

Spirit of the Earth.—The flaming mountain is a valve in the earth's surface, whereby release of pressure can be achieved. The coating of water or moisture which covers the fiery core of our planet, brings constant pressure to bear upon the unstable forces within, which requires adjustment and release from period to period. Even the planetary spirit (Spirit of the Earth) is having his evolution changed by the fate that has come upon him and the mantle of water that surrounds him. Instead of being given over to the lower aspects of material fire and the destructive forces which could manifest here, he is becoming green and verdant and fertile, capable of good as well as of evil, or rather of growth instead of mere energy.

Mixing of Evolutions.—Demons are pure energy, as yet unguided and uncontrolled. They are the early aspects of force, issued forth from the infinite, but as yet unevolved. In them lies the germ of power, and in time their growth will clothe them with the garments of restraint, and they will find much useful labour to accomplish. But when they contact evolutions already advanced, they can be only destructive, like lightning in a tool shop. It has been the mixing of evolutions here that has caused confusion—the contact too early with human evolutions before the demons were mellowed, and the ignorant association with humans before the time when they could be governed.

It is unfortunate for the demons, too, to step out of their evolution and to take on semblance of human actions before the due time. They are like children provided with edged tools, before they can safely use them.

Certain humans who evolve to the point of power and prove destructive are cast back into the furnace, as it were to be re-cast. They are thrown back into the demon evolution to learn again the primary lessons in which they have failed. This is eonic damnation. And the escape of these erstwhile humans while they have yet to be purified to mingle again too soon with human evolution is destructive to themselves and to those with whom they associate yet escape was often made possible by Atlantean magic.

Semi-human Entities.—It was these semi-human entities that the black magicians of Atlantis summoned to assist them in their wars, and the misguided entities had much labour for naught and were set back again at the primary lessons. It was because of this that Jesus at times showed consideration for demons, because he knew their association with humans was due to human interference, and that it spelled disaster for the unfortunate demons wrested from their prison before they were prepared. It has been the effort of many occultists to persuade these demons to retire voluntarily from human association and return to their habitat until they were thoroughly griddled and mellowed by heat and tempered for their work.

Some of them it has been necessary to imprison on the

planet. They have progressed too far towards humanity. For these, cell-like prisons are built and they are encased like a caddis so that they can do no more damage. Here they await in peace the day of release when they can be sent to a humanity suited to their needs. Some, however, have entered so far into human evolution that they cannot be sealed, but at the hour of judgment must be sent rapidly away for the protection of the rest of humanity, and undergo once more the ancient penance pronounced long ago. They will enter into a new group of demons to endeavor in the long slow process of mellowing to learn wisdom, sacrifice and restraint.

Imprisoned Souls.—Through many ages the planet has progressed towards peace. It will be achieved, and in time some beneficent influence will enter also into the tortured and tempestuous souls who dwell within our sphere, beings, remember, etheric only in form, and therefore beings affected not unduly by the heat, but victims rather of their own turbulent spirits which must be mellowed ere they can be freed. How restless they are to move, to do, to act, to destroy, to rend anything for action!

Hells.—Those who suffer are those confined with them who remember other conditions, but who must share the penance of disobedience; one group disobedient as yet because untrained—the other disobedient through intention. It is the latter who are spoken of in the various myths about hell. Some are indeed encased in ice in the frozen North. These are the souls who diverted creative fire and contacted some degree of eternal life, and must wear out their doom in inaction before they can again be set to work. Here they remain harmless until the fire they stole for their own purposes has worn itself out and the souls fall once more under the laws of life and death.

DEMONIC FORCES AND BATTLING HOSTS

Invasions of Disease.—The demonic forces are objectified on the physical plane by the pests and plagues. A constant struggle against these is necessary, and against the invasions of disease, another aspect of the demonic forces. Animals are no more immune than men. It is part of the heritage of this planet. But gradually forces are being developed which can conquer these invasions of disease. Electricity, light, colour, all playing upon the etheric, will strengthen it so that it can resist invasion of the physical, and gradually rarify the atoms to the point where they cannot respond to the lower destructive forces. Knowledge of the forces of X-ray and electricity, will bring an end to troubles of this kind. This knowledge is part of the heritage of the new age, and the gift of our new Star Ruler. There are already beings upon the planet whom insects do not bite, and in time disease also will not attack.

Cleansing of Evil Areas.—The battling hosts are cleansing many evil areas. There is a vast amount of work still to be done. One reason for the disclosure of so many buried and forgotten civilizations is to help cleanse out the evil entities left there during the decadence. Desolation and sand covered the ancient iniquities, and the old sites were abandoned by men as the only protection from evil. Now the whole world must be cleansed and ancient tombs are opened and aired, and the ancient evil destroyed. Egypt is being opened up, and Yucatan and Mexico. All sites of ancient civilizations must be found and cleansed. Many evil entities hover over the sands and can only be exorcised by the aid of sun and water.

Hatred Has Its Purpose

Hatred has its purpose. Hymns of hate and paeans of joy are both expressions of intensity—one of hate, one of love. And both serve to bring man forward out of the sluggish miasma in which he dwells. These two almost equally intensify the action of the molecules, and set his slow vehicles to throbbing. It is the tensing of the wire, the tightening of the bow-string that the arrow may at last fly swift and sure to its destination. Nay, more: hatred is the force which rouses man to trample his lower nature beneath him. Righteous indignation fights against oppression and injustice. It has been the great force against evil and corruption and degradation, into which civilization after civilization fell.

Now, hatred is the product of the demons. Nor can it be spared from any evolution. An ingredient which may be dangerous in its pure form, when mixed with other elements gives a useful product. So with hatred, and so too with demons. When their first fierce energy in its destructive form is curbed, they may mingle in evolutions and become the motive power of growth. A child is destructive because he expresses almost pure energy, untempered by wisdom or understanding. All he desires is to use his power on conditions about him to express the bubbling energy within him in any form, and because he does not know enough to be constructive, he is destructive. It is the first expression of energy. Only when energy is governed by intellect and controlled in expression by knowledge, does it cease to be destructive. Lightning is ungoverned energy. Electricity is energy tempered by intelligence to constructive use.

Hatred, then, has its place, as have demons. But these must be governed, controlled and directed in their expression.

V · DEVA EVOLUTION

V · DEVA EVOLUTION

EVOLUTION THROUGH HARMONY

There are other evolutions connected with this planet besides the demon and the human. Something remains to be said about the Deva, an evolution also undergoing unusual conditions in connection with their growth here. It is customary for the Deva world to evolve through harmony—music, beauty, obedience, purity and love. It is not usual for them to be summoned to meet opposing and destructive forces, to find conflict and combat in their work. Yet all these things are happening upon this planet, and therefore the Devas, too, are taking on characteristics which normally do not belong to their point of development.

Some Enter Human Kingdom.—Just as men have taken on through association some part of the demon nature, so Devas have taken on some part of the human nature. They are developing will and power as well as love and devotion. It is this admixture of qualities, primarily human, that has permitted some Devas to enter into our humanity and actually undertake human evolution long before their time. Man has been likened to the Prodigal Son, and the Deva to the Faithful Son; to some extent the analogy is true.

In any case, certain of the more courageous and advanced Devas have filtered into human bodies and shared the Karmic pains and penalties. These, however, have been

95

prepared by loyal service in meeting and opposing the demonic hordes. So here in this planet many evolutions have mingled. Hence the great contrasts and the great disparities in character.

Yet, in the end, probably most if not all of the three evolutions will have their development hastened by the contacts which have arisen through coincident residence upon this planet and this series of chains.

A few of the demons who have been liberated from imprisonment too early will suffer, but in the end they, too, will have the Karmic regard for those who liberated them when they have at last risen beyond the sorrows and sins of humanity; they will have it as their obligation to assist and succour those whom they injured in long past times. The law is intricate and complex, but very just.

CREATION OF DEVA BODIES

It is sometimes thought that Devas are here to supervise certain phases of kingdoms of nature. But Devas live just as humans live, and their duties are merely activities incidental to that living. They have their birth, growth and death, just as humans, plants and worlds, not so fraught with pain as is human life, but with definite periods, none the less. When the time comes for a new incarnation, they choose the line and experience which seems best suited to their unfoldment, and cause a body to be created for their purposes. This is accomplished by ceremonial magic on the inner planes by choristers of song, by trumpeters and musicians in a musical crescendo of power and harmony.

WHERE DEVAS ROAM, THERE GROWS BEAUTY

Their Habitats.—Where Devas choose their habitat and roam, there grows beauty. There nature manifests itself in transcendent form. In deep woods, near running streams, in wide meadows, flower strewn, on stern mountain slopes majestic in form, in gardens gay with colour, there dwell Devas. And their presence is made almost tangible by a quality of personality in the scene about, a sense of brooding peace or of leaping joy or of tranquil delight that seems to greet one like a presence or a voice.

They choose their habitats much as humans do, according to temperament or taste. Some brood over ocean caves, some over rocky promontories. Although they do not manifest upon the physical plane normally, yet this plane creates an atmosphere, a condition to which they respond. For there is a reality about form and place, which can be felt on all planes connected with it. For physical form is really just a more complete crystallization of a solution. In essence, both crystal and solution must remain similar. Consider form as a densification of any given element, not a changed formula. This means that form and spirit are merely opposite poles of the same thing; one in rarified form, one having reached the crystallized state.

Connection Between Worlds.—Therefore, a great mountain here corresponds to a centre of power in the inner worlds. It is the outward and manifest form of an inner reality. There is closer connection between the worlds than many realize. There is stronger connection between the physical body and the spirit than most understand. And it is only through the gateway of the physical that ultimate salvation and achievement can be reached.

In the past, emphasis has been placed upon rising into the inner worlds and renouncing the physical. Two reasons for this existed. First, despair and defeat was the Dharma of physical life, only to be endured by focusing elsewhere. Secondly, the grip of the physical element was so powerful that men must be taught to look up and free themselves, because so only could they rise out of it.

New Laws.—But conditions have changed. The era of the downward drag of the physical is past. The arc has been turned, and matter itself is springing upward. As in each civilization new laws and new aspects of religion must be unfolded to meet a different need, so today, as a new world presses into being, new understanding and new laws must govern evolution. It is idle to look to the past for present guidance. The past can give some of the history of evolution, and some of the methods of past evolution, and some fundamental laws. But the true teaching must spring from the requirements of the future.

Conquest of Matter.—Today, the earth and the world are becoming spiritualized. The religion of the future will link physical with spiritual; will find its highest summation in expression on the physical plane. The earth and its ways, its laws, its civilizations must be carried upward, not denied, and a heaven upon earth established. This shall be the true conquest of matter. Man at last escapes its grip and begins to soar upward to his own place. But he must carry with him this sheath of matter which was established for him.

Understand, the core of the planet will remain unchanged; but all those atomic structures which were sent for man's protection—that sheath of water and greenery, its cells and atoms, must be raised with man. What will happen, will be that the cells will become rarefied at last, that they will function only on the etheric, and the earth will become less dense, its core perhaps the same, but surrounded by sheaths of vapour, not dense matter.

When this happens, man will be freed from insect life which cannot function there, and he will create his foods from the ethers, living largely upon mist vapour and perfumes. His children will be created as the Devas are, by ectoplasm drawn from the bodies of the parents; literally a materialization brought about with the help of a group of harmonious spirits, who form a magnetic ring within which the forces can safely work.

So, once more, the race will grow and create by oozing or budding. The arc swings back to its original place at last.

THE RANKS OF THE DEVAS

Newly Evolving Souls.—The ranks of the Devas are filled by newly evolving souls from its various preliminary kingdoms. Evolution through the lower kingdoms of earth is much swifter among Devas than with humans, because their habitat or true centre will not be the physical plane but the higher planes, and they need, therefore, less preparation than is required for the physical plane. Their atoms will not be exposed to the terrific impacts of human life, and require, accordingly, less preparatory impacts—a shorter period of ingestion.

In fact, only those Devas who are to be connected directly with work on the physical plane, on its higher etheric levels, ever take physical form, among birds, fishes and reptiles who are connected with their evolution. They evolve usually through the four elements as nature spirits, contacting the human plane at an earlier stage as a tiny algae for a comparatively short period only. Then they transfer rapidly onward to the higher levels.

Star Angels.—Certain Star Angels or Beings connected with the Star Angel retinues, who decide upon human incarnation (it greatly facilitates work if the servers can enter incarnation occasionally for special service, and this cannot be done until they have passed through some of the preliminary stages here), take occasional incarnations in the lower kingdoms, just sufficient to prepare a permanent physical atom. As said before, the Star Angels are all Beings who have human experience elsewhere, so they can recapitulate rapidly the evolutionary arc.

Some prepare to enter the Deva kingdom; some prepare also for the human; some enter the human alone. To enter the human kingdom only, requires incarnation in some of the greater animals as a preliminary. To contact also the Deva kingdoms, experience in each of the four nature kingdoms is needful.

Battling Devas.—Among the Devas, there is one great unique group, the battling Devas, the Warrior Lords. These beings have so evolved that they can combat evil forces. They are drawn from the Avenging Angels, who deal with destruction and death. They are akin to fire and have so transmuted their natures that they can face evil in man and in demon, and become the Guardian Wall of the planetary humans.

Avenging Angels.—These Avenging Angels were obliged to enter into physical form. They chose the snake and the dragon or crocodile, a poor descendant of the dragon. Only so could they develop rapidly the combative force needed for their work. It is for this reason that tradition holds the serpent and the crocodile sacred, because they are degenerate descendants of forms used by the Warrior Devas. In Egypt these Warrior Devas helped to guard secrets from the black magicians and the Serpent of Egypt symbolized on the forehead of the Pharaoh the power to invoke these guardian spirits for the protection of his race.

CLASSES OF DEVAS

Warrior Lords and Court Choristers.—The Devas group themselves into different classes. Some follow the Warrior Lords and learn a new line of development. Some enter the higher worlds and become court choristers, by their continuous music keeping the vibrations of peace and joy coursing powerfully about the courts of the Star Lords. These echo the music of the spheres.

Some supervise the development of the lower kingdoms and the unfoldment of nature on the planet. Some control the winds and the great magnetic currents that belt the earth.

Devas of the Nations.—Then there are the Devas of the nations, with their attendants, and the Devas of certain magnetized areas. Deva life has some parallels to human life. They have their chosen habitats, and there they refresh and revivify themselves after their labours. They revivify themselves in various ways, but one is to bathe in certain magnetic areas, where sun or water or both are especially pure and active. Winds, too, help them, or rather the magnetic etheric conditions left by winds if not too intense. Great waterfalls and wide lakes delight them, and wooded mountain sides and sparkling mountain streams; also, high glaciers and snowy mountain peaks.

Nature Kingdoms.—The nature kingdoms for the most part do little more than live in their appointed elements. Until they have graduated from the four elements, they are given little work. But once they pass out of the purely elemental kingdoms, their intelligence increases and they enter into more definite labours. While members of one of the four elements, they are really only sharing the life of that element and learning to incorporate the atoms into their vehicles. They are in the condition of human egos functioning in the three elemental kingdoms prior to the mineral.

But in each of the four elements, or connected therewith, are nature spirits who have learned to control and use the elemental force of one group. These are conscious intelligent entities who govern the forces for the planet and who are leaders, guides and teachers of the more child-like elemental groups. As was said, Devas pass through the earlier stages more rapidly than men.

Minor Devas.—When they begin to have a larger individual consciousness, they enter forms with specific duties. Such are the flower fairies, the gnomes, the elves, and certain other fairy kingdoms. Then, too, there are the minor Devas, larger than these small folk but nevertheless of low intelligence and merely servitors to their leaders. It is often these who confuse and mislead humans. They are like mischievous children.

THE BATTLING DEVAS

Ring-Pass-Not.—When the battling Devas go forth, they go to protect the planet from invasion. Normally, every planet has its ring-pass-not, which protects it from wandering troups of rebellious entities. But this cinder has not this protection. Its ring-pass-not has been formed by the authority and will of the Star Angels. Remember, when speaking of the planet, the whole chain is referred to, not merely this present planet; yes, and the series of incarnations belonging to this chain. The climax, however, is only now approaching. There are many strange things in this evolution, contrary to the usual laws.

Duties.—Among the battling Devas, there are varying groups and offices. Some guard the outer ring of the earth. Some guard the chain, some guard special nations, locations and even individuals. The invocation of a guardian angel was taught in the church ceremonies, because the church had knowledge of evil, and understanding of it, and recognized established means of protection. Today we rebel against the horrors taught children in folk and fairy tale, but they embody the necessary tradition of the race and are based upon fact.

Overcoming Evil.—But as the world progresses and law replaces lawlessness, and peace replaces war, and obedience, chaos, the time is coming where it is no longer needful to be in fear. The means of cleansing evil is to force it from the inner plane to the physical and there overcome it. So, much is being precipitated to the physical plane and there conquered. This accounts for the strange and terrible outbreaks of crime and cruelty everywhere, especially in

America. Each land must be cleansed but the greatest battle is actually in progress here now.

ALLIES OF THE DEVAS

Symbols and Sacrifice.—The allies of the Deva world have been drawn from many sources and have thrown their energies into helping the Devas in their labours. The old Hindu rite of offering rice to the Devas had in it a definite purpose of assisting them in their protective work. The rice itself was but a symbol, and acted as a tangible stimulus to the will offering, which was the real value. Tangible symbols have been used throughout the childhood of the race to embody great and occult truths. The bread and wine of the sacrament is indeed a true symbol of the body and blood which Jesus offered to appease the wrath of the demonic forces, and when devotees used the symbol, they definitely drew down the benediction established for their protection in the great reservoirs, by the actual sacrifice of Jesus, of His body and blood for man. In other words, the church has been nearer the truth than latter-day theorists have believed. Again and again in ancient legend, good has been wrested from the demons for the race by actual living sacrifice. Odin sacrificed an eye. Prometheus was a constant sacrifice. Even the legends of Andromeda were true. Sacrifice alone at certain terrible periods kept down the destructive forces of the evil ones.

Many strange things occurred before man came into his power and began, through intelligence, to conquer the destructive aspect of nature. Yet he came into his heritage only after the intolerable sacrifices of the leaders had cleansed him enough to prepare him safely to wield its powers.

Orgies of Atlantis.—The orgies of Atlantis were demonic, and in some way loosed fiends from their imprisonment. If men were willing to lend their bodies to the demons for a period, the contact with human life and blood in some way gave the fiends an anchor which permitted them to remain near the earth upon its surface. During the period that they inhabited the obsessed bodies, they drew in something of the vital prana, and if they could induce orgies of a cannibalistic nature, the actual absorption of human blood gave them material from which to form a semi-dense human form. This in an indirect way is the cause of parasites who suck human blood or animal blood. Their existence is due to the reducing of semi-embodied fiends into form to lessen their menace, and to the perpetuation of the instinct for blood which vitalizes the whole group soul.

During the dark ages, one of the problems has been that those who had been temple seers, unprotected, have fallen victim to evil influences, become obsessed and such horrors as the Inquisition resulted.

Devas Assisted by Humans.—To turn now to the contemplation of pleasanter things, the Devas have the help of many humans, and also the nature kingdoms, which have been established to guard the growth of beauty upon earth. These little people are friendly, and help all who turn to them in friendly spirit and who show little of the demonic influence. More and more these elves and undines, sylphs and salamanders will co-operate with humanity. These kingdoms have been established as primary groups for the Deva evolution, as animals have been as primary groups for the human. Neither really belonged upon this fiery cinder, and it is only because a great and gracious Presence enveloped earth with a watery atmosphere that the pleasantness of our habitation has been possible upon this planet. This great presence was the Mother of Waters who cast her mantle over our system of chains, when humanity entered upon the fulfillment of its doom.

THE LORE OF THE DEVAS

Opposed by Demon Forces.—The lore of the Devas is not given to men, lest they damage themselves by misuse of it. Some portions will now become available for the few. It has been said that Devas, on being summoned here to assist man, found themselves opposed by demon forces. The major part of these demons exist in the earth but portions are let loose from time to time by seismic disturbances, earthquakes and volcanoes. These form avenues of escape to the outer world, and once free, the demons hide in corners of the planet most suited to their temperaments, and thwart and torture humans and animals. It has been the part of the Shining Ones to shelter man from these demonic influences, and to seek to segregate and to control them. In this, they have been helped by the church services which put force at their command. Services in the various religions throughout the years have invoked the good and exorcised the evil forces.

Avenues of Escape.—Unfortunately, men from time to time have learned of these demonic orders, and have sought to avail themselves of their powers. Therefore, they have sometimes opened avenues of escape into the world, in return for promises of wealth or revenge or what-not. These promises have been kept, but frequently the fulfillment of the promises has wrought disaster later upon the man who exacted them.

Protective Measures.—In the meantime, efforts have been made to protect men from these savage beings. Holy centres have been established into which they could not effectively penetrate. They have been incarcerated and rendered harmless, as in the tales of Solomon. They have been restricted to certain areas where they could do the least damage. But, with the closing of the temples five thousand years ago, and the limiting of the electric Sirian force on the planet preparatory to the dark ages, much less control of these demons was possible. And mankind fell more and more under their influence. In order to use the destructive force at work in the world as wisely as possible, men were encouraged to enter great wars of conquest and adventure. Here the destruction was mitigated by the lessons of obedience and sacrifice and endurance gained.

THE BEAUTY OF WISDOM

The beauty of wisdom lies in the eternity of truth. Wisdom is simple. Truth is simple. Law is simple. Complexity comes only in variety of expression, in confusion of manifestation, like the pieces of a picture puzzle, looked at separately. Yet when once united into a whole, the theme is clear and confusion disappears. So it is with life. When consciousness can span a great enough arc of time, the plan becomes clear. It is the narrow limits of a finite mind grappling with a tiny segment of history that cause confusion.

Wisdom is closely associated with beauty. Intellect consists of the grasp of component parts. Wisdom is the vision which comes from uniting them and finding beauty. Beauty is a divine gift, more closely associated with certain aspects of the Trinity and with certain types of force. It reacts directly upon certain centres in the brain, more susceptible in some individuals and in some races than others. Beauty is more closely associated with the solar plexus and the instinctive system than with the brain, and reacts more forcibly, therefore, upon women and upon fourth race types, than upon men and fifth race types. It actually feeds certain nerve centres. It is one reason for the strange fascination for women of jewels and beautiful fabrics and colours. Artists in all lines, who are linked with the Deva Kingdom, have similar responses. Women suffer more than men from the impacts of our modern ugly utilitarian civilization, and the coming influence of women is seen in the increase of colour and beauty in our cities and commodites. It is well known that woman's eye is more responsive to colour and that she rarely suffers from colour blindness.

Certain magnetic influences pour out from beauty, and women will be less nervous and less irritable when beauty surrounds them. Men are more responsive to comfort, women to beauty.

Assistants in Man's Redemption.—You have done us great service in the past, many of you, in entering into the problems of the shining world, the Deva world, and easing our labours. We are the good fairies who seek ever to lessen the evil done to man by the curses of the evil beings. We, too, have our problems and our tribulations. Sent here to assist in man's redemption, we have found ourselves at war with the earlier denizens of the planet, demon souls incarcerated here for special tempering.

These have yet thousands of centuries to endure in their troubled prisons. "Devils in the underworlds work out the sins of ages past." This is the eternal damnation, the imprisonment within the earth at its fiery core, where they seethe and rage and torment themselves and one another. Here at last they will be burned free, or will be reduced to impotency and return to the elements from which they were drawn, to become again, in the direst cases, earth, air, fire and water and to dissipate the danger of accumulated misapplied power in the disintegration into cellular life.

Man's Fall

Man came by error into that abode where devils were incarcerated. He fell onto the surface of a sphere which boiled within with the accumulated malice of eons, sent here, to the densest sphere, where he could do least harm. Within the earth is indeed hell, and the fire of eonic punishment. Man's own evil nature and deeds have permitted the escape of some of those in prison. He loosed these to feed his own passions, and they have turned and rent him limb from limb. Some of the evil of the inner hell expresses itself upon the surface of the planet in verminous life, not related to man and his kingdoms, and ever at war with him and his legions of the damned. Ensouling vermin, rodents, pestiferous insects, snakes, spiders and the like; even in the sea, are escaped demons in monster form, still savage and horrifying.

THE GREAT RIVER LORD

Rivers have mighty consciousnesses, truly like great Devas. The Lord of a mighty river is a very potent Being, usually beneficent and friendly, but capable of being roused by warfare or turmoil into a human menace. Water is a great purifier and cleanser, and the larger rivers are swarming with nature spirits and fairy folk and Devas who carry joy and cleanliness and well-being to the people along the river banks. No wonder natives of all countries love their rivers. They are the milk of the World Mother, poured out for their benefit. Running water and fresh water have a peculiar quality of their own. They are almost the essence of spiritual beneficence, of healing and purifying powers. They feed, nourish and sustain all life and are filled alike with physical prana and spiritual stimulation.

In time, much can be accomplished by invoking the power of the River God for mankind's help and in the case of some of the sacred rivers, such as the Ganges, Wise Ones in the past have done this very thing and established a healing centre for their people. Through powerful magic and wise form-building, channels of etheric power have been built for the distribution of healing, and many have been served.

THE DEVA SONG

Sing, oh ye Devas of the morn! Sing of the joy which hovers about the planet as the hour of redemption approaches. Long has man sojourned in the place of death, hidden by the black clouds of Karmic debt from the effulgence of God's Presence. Despairing, bitter, distraught, led by faith in some ultimate release, man by his courage has endured the pangs of hell. Long ages rolled, lightened only by the faith of the few who preached release and the goodness of the Father and the way of achievement by renunciation. In darkness the people stumbled onward. In darkness they were born, lived and died.

Now, after many eons, dawns the day. Through the murk which surrounds our spiritual progress, the first clear rays of the coming light appear along the horizon. The spiritual Sun long hid from man, which assured well-being, peace and joy, soon will rise in the East to usher in the new day.

Minor Day of Judgment.—The Minor Day of Judgment is in progress. Souls are tried and tested, judged worthy or found wanting. With this new day, those that cannot lay aside the trappings of their earth-born natures must pass out and await another chance for their atonement. But the others who have won the light shall receive the light, and our darkened planet shall once more take its place among the company of Heaven, in radiant garb of light.

VI · THE COSMIC EVOLUTION

VI · THE COSMIC EVOLUTION

THE COSMIC SCHEME

Why Planets Differ.—In the far reaches of the heavens are many evolutions. These evolve different qualities of soul. And as one finds in this humanity varied types—musicians, artists, builders, business men, clowns, poets, teachers, mothers, students and philosophers—so one finds in the cosmic evolutions those who are specializing in various powers, faculties or characters. If once one grasps this fully, one can understand why planets differ, and why humanities have varying paths to follow. Even on this planet it is rare for one soul to contact more than a few possible lines of development, even in the course of many lives. He could not achieve the superior craftsmanship which will be needed in his work after leaving this planet, if he sought to encompass too many lines at once. The powers he requires for his future work must be fully unfolded and this can only be accomplished by repeated efforts along a single line until, through conflict with circumstances, effort and struggle, the powers of soul are matured.

The great mass of humanity are following one major bent and its branches. There are here in incarnation a few specialists, often come here from other evolutions, either to develop some side quality they need, or to take, as it were, a post-graduate course here in their own specialty, to gain a few new angles of vision upon it.

Humanity's Major Trend.—As a whole, however, humanity has one major trend and that is the use and control of the destructive forces of the universe, wisely and efficiently. These destructive forces can be a very powerful aid to evolution, if controlled and directed into proper channels. Indeed always before any new work can be accomplished, destruction of the old and a general cleansing of conditions is necessary. Moreover, in a more individual way human souls cannot evolve unless they are tempered and tried. This can be done only by pain, suffering, anguish or sorrow, mental, emotional and physical. The forces which accomplish this must be wisely directed, to gain the maximum of effect with the minimum of pain, and so planned that they will not wreck the vehicles. This last is a peculiarly difficult matter, and only those blessed with great compassion and love and understanding can be entrusted with these tester forces. Unless they can understand and sympathize themselves with the pain endured, they cannot be trusted to know the danger point, and if it approaches suddenly, to ease the pressure and reverse the currents so that the candidate is flooded with love, joy and peace for a measurable period, until the saturation point of strain is passed.

Distortion in Humanity.—It has been said that this planet is developing the devils and torturers for the cosmic scheme. This is true, and these torturers in time will pass through some form of humanity like ours, learn compassion in highest degree, and become the administrators of pain. In the case of this planet, humanity became too deeply involved in matter, and too closely associated with the inner kingdoms of the planet, and themselves took on some of the attributes of the impersonal elementals who were evolving along this particular line. This accounts for the horrible distortions in humanity. It was never intended that humans should practice cruelties upon each other, but on the contrary that, driven by a common fate, they should learn their interdependence, and from this, compassion, tenderness and mutual sacrifice. They have slipped back into a dire condition and humans now have to meet not only the dangers of elementals, but the terrible disaster of human cruelty.

This took place in its worst form on this planet in the Atlantean days, and at that time thousands of powerful and terrible elementals were formed, having gained life from sacrificed humans, the elemental life of whom they actually built into themselves so that they would endure for long periods. The makers of these elemental monsters—Frankensteins—used that terrible and sacred and potent force residing in human blood, to accomplish their purposes. It is only now that we are able to destroy some of them, now that the Sirian force has again been loosed on the planet and the electrical forces again put at the service of mankind. Remember always that a terrible *fall* has occurred and two kingdoms have thus become interwoven to the disaster of both; hence, the early teachings against *magic* which was largely the creation of elementals for selfish and destructive purposes.

THE HEAVENLY CHOIRS OF ANGELS

Life Forces.—The heavenly choirs of angels actually exist and function at appointed periods for specific purposes. These heavenly choirs form a link between the lowest worlds and the highest. They keep active the flow of the life forces through the planes and between sphere and sphere. They are the life blood of the inner worlds and carry the pranic currents into all parts of the cosmic organisms.

There is a close relation between the functions of a human body and the functions of a cosmic system. There are strange similarities throughout. Much is yet unknown about the play of finer forces through a human body, magnetism, vitality, blood circulation and clarification. But in time these things will become clearer as man adds to his power of sight and thought.

Planetary Blood System.—The Devas correspond to the white blood corpuscles; the mass of humanity, to the red. The Devas function in caring for the well-being of the planet as a whole, acting under direct orders, like the sympathetic system, and fulfilling their mission, one might say, involuntarily. Man corresponds to the cerebro-spinal system and to the red cells, and acts under conscious impulse for the uses he plans for the body.

The white corpuscles fight the invasion of foreign and inimical entities. The red corpuscles carry food to the organisms. In the same way, Devas fight the invading hordes of destroyers that constantly seek to enter the planet, and men provide the physical labour which provides food for humanity and which supplies also the life-giving impulses to the development of the animal and vegetable kingdoms. Evolution in both animal and vegetable kingdoms depends upon the interposition of man and his intelligent direction and analysis.

LORDS OF THE FLAME

The angels of fire do not descend to the physical plane. They contact only the mental, and pass their power over antahkarana to form the link between the lower and the higher selves. At initiation they are invoked to widen the slender bridge which was made at individualization. They represent the true creative fire, and are linked to the Third Aspect of the Logos, material fire and activity and mind, Lords of The Flame, Lords of Mind.

Behind the aspects of fire lie many powers which are most potent on the inner planes but less suited to the physical and emotional. Pure flame finally purifies the lower vehicles of all dross, but until that purification is accomplished in the seventh round—when the inner flames will shine clear, through transparent, unclouded, stabilized vehicles—purity must be attained by pain. Pain is the material aspect of flame. Flame purifies by intensifying the speed of the molecules until they vibrate red hot and become, as it were, incandescent. As the material body is too dense to endure such rarification and heating, a slower method is used which intensifies more slowly and does not endanger the cohesive power of the molecules.

In time man will indeed enter the fire to be purified but not until the water content of his body has been greatly reduced and the matter rarefied. When the body is over-keyed, water reduces the rapidity of action of the atoms, used either inside or out.

Flame plays a great part in the evolution of the future. Cold flame or crystallized flame is electricity, and this will be used to rarefy bodies in the future and so avoid so great a need for pain. The bodies can be rarefied rapidly now, by a lighter diet—no meat, alcohol or tobacco. It may interest you to know that smoking is a means of killing out the action of meat upon the body, of reducing hatred, fierceness and cruelty, also passion, and that it is preparing the way for the vegetarian diet, which is coming rapidly. Smoke is poison to sensitive bodies, as it reduces the atomic activity and throws the solar plexus out of gear. But it is, nevertheless, a means to a great end—the lesser evil. It will bridge the gap for many hyper-sensitive bodies, between their own vibration and that of the world they live in, by slowing them down to fit the coarser vibration, and make life endurable.

Those who raise their vibrations to lead the race to new heights will need to live away from congested city centres and the intensified magnetic aura of lower humans found about cities. Rural communities must be formed where these advanced groups can live.

EXPERIMENTAL GROUNDS

Manifestations of Life.—Vast areas in the Cosmic Scheme are experimental grounds for ways and means of perfecting life, or the manifestation of life, so that beings may become more powerful, more joyous, more beautiful, with every new outpouring of life into manifestation. Manifestation occurs because the vital force needs expression. It cannot remain inactive more than a period. It leaps forward to new endeavours, new expressions, new beauties, new understandings, as eagerly as a youth goes forth on voyages of exploration.

Purpose of Life.—The purpose of life is joy and fulfillment in achievement. The joy lies in the novelty and the ingenuity of the plan and the final accomplishment, not in the immediate detail.

For all forms of life are but temporary expressions of an effort to surpass in joyous competition each earlier manifestation of form. This must become clear. Life and growth need not be attended by pain, but by the vigorous interest and the joy of a happy childhood. Joy in daily tasks skilfully performed, joy in nature all flow from the spring of vital force in a normal and natural way.

PAIN—THE GREAT GUIDE OF HUMANITY

Above the storm and stress of human life lies the enfolding atmosphere of peace. It is this of which the prophet speaks, the peace which passeth understanding, and it is to this that all souls aspire. When once they can break through the miasmas of the lower airs, when once they can reach upward in spirit to the eternal ranges of being and there dwell, the peace of God enters their souls and abideth there. Then have they fulfilled the purposes of human struggle. Then turn they back to give blind humanity, still mazed and groping, that spiritual peace which alone brings contentment and lasting happiness.

Pain is the great guide of humanity from the treacherous bogs of the lower worlds of consciousness; pain, the great purifier, man's most tender, most compassionate guide. It acts as the spur which goads the panting horse to leap the dark and dangerous chasm. So pain, anguish, grief, despair, bereavement, challenge the soul of man to look beyond the planes of earthly life for happiness, for peace, for beauty, and for joy. Happiness comes not through dumb submission, by the breaking and humbling of the spirit, by resignation unlighted by joy. It comes by will, tempered to endurance and to power by pain; by the resolution to find the abode of light, the place of peace beyond the storm-ridden world of men.

It is the purpose of the new race to achieve this goal for the mass of the people. They must glimpse its reality, even if they cannot at all times vision the full realization of it.

PRAYER

Answers to Prayer.—The subject to be discussed is that of prayer, in its relation to man, and in its relation to the releasing of cosmic force. Prayer has been instituted in the universe by certain beneficent Beings who realized man's hapless and hopeless lot, and who have sought to mitigate his distress. Answers to prayer come not from the Supreme Source of Being, as many believe, but from intermediaries, either of a Deva, human or super-human origin. These Beings have established systems to meet the desperate need of humans when coping with forces too powerful or too onerous for their strength. There are, first, reservoirs of force which can be tapped, and then agents who may invoke this force for the protection and succour of unfortunate and deserving humans. The Catholic church, which teaches its people to appeal to the Saints, is nearer the truth than most Protestants realize, for the Saints are often enrolled in volunteer groups for such service. There is a great body of Catholic entities in the higher worlds who have built up a powerful organization to reply to the deserving prayers of people.

Agencies.—The instrument of prayer has been established to assist humans in keeping faith during the darkest periods of human evolution. It appears in all religions for the simpler folk, and offers them sanctuary from intolerable pressure upon mind and heart. In addition to the ordinary group of Saints and Super-Human Beings, there are regular orders of Devas who have undertaken to spare part of their energies to the service of men in the answering of prayer. There are many agencies at work, and help is brought in various ways, by tapping reservoirs and increasing the strength and endurance of the individual, by attracting the attention of other humans through suggestion and guiding them to the place of need, by actually interposing a sheltering wall when humans are in danger, by turning power upon the menace and bringing terror to it—as in the case of wild beasts dangerous men. It is to be remembered, however, that only race Karma may thus be diverted—not personal Karma. This is an important point. Karma, which is the result of race ignorance, can be lifted—not Karma which comes as a personal equalization of egoic debt. Healing comes under this grouping, it being the interposition of semi-divine Beings to benefit deserving individuals and to foster faith in divine or super-human agencies.

Effective Prayer.—Prayer to be effective must so intensify the body that it becomes highly sensitized, and therefore responsive to the finer forces. It must be ardent, and either anguished or ecstatic, to put the body into a properly receptive condition. The intensity forms a funnel through which force may be received, and through the release of will, flashes out like a signal light upon the inner planes and arouses the attention of some watcher. It is not so different from conditions upon the physical planes, where desperate cries of one in trouble arouse the attention of the passer-by and cause him to give aid.

Special Protectors.—Certain individuals who have earned it are given special guards and protectors who watch over them in times of danger. Certain seers of the inner planes who can foresee something of approaching dangers keep a general watch over considerable groups of valued workers, and when they see danger imminent, send out guards to protect them, just as a police station sends out officers in response to a call for help—except in this case the call comes from the seer, who foresees the danger, and not from the individual who is in need.

Places of Refuge.—One should remember that the Paradises and Heavens were established by kindly Beings who saw humanity's plight and made these places of refuge for use and refreshment between incarnations. All evolutions do not have them as they are not needed. They are like the cities of refuge in the Bible. It is for this reason that many workers can and do refuse to accept the vacation in the face of the great need of the world. They are not required parts of evolution but established as rest havens—established long after evolution was well advanced.

This planet must solve its own problems and win its own salvation through the efforts of its people and the volunteers. Just as a great financier might visit a city and find dire need for a hospital and establish it, so volunteers and some of the great visiting Lords out of their own bounty have established these havens of rest and reservoirs of beneficent power.

Naturally, their powers also are limited, and help is

given only in measure as man can receive and use it. Some cannot be helped by what is available; hence the healing of some and not of others. It is determined by many different conditions not to be fully discussed now. It is too complex a problem.

Avenues of Light.—Avenues of light are being opened through the darkness of the atmosphere of this planet, and many beneficent influences are pouring in. But this is the result of personal efforts on the part of some humans and volunteers who have established friendly relations with Lords of other planets and are gaining good for their people through these relations. Again, the simile holds of a charity worker, who through his personal efforts reaches the ear of a great man and invokes help in establishing hospitals for his people.

THE DOCTRINE OF THE ATONEMENT

Sacrifice to Nullify Evil.—The outcome of these protracted efforts will indeed be salvation for those who avail themselves of it, and judgment and banishment for those who continue to show forth rebellion and malice. There is more in the doctrine of the atonement than many realize.

One of the ways in which the malicious forces could be counteracted was by voluntary sacrifice. The blood of human beings shed to help the world in some strange way nullifies the evil on the planet. We are indeed cleansed by the blood of the Lambs of God. Jesus of Nazareth ushered in this darkest age by the example of sacrifice. This has been the darkest age, because the spiritual lamps have been hooded and men's minds have been confused by ignorance and doubt. The beams of spiritual light could no longer penetrate the gloom and even the wise ones found their path by faith alone, or by the light won by personal efforts. The triumph of the destructive hosts was held back by the actual blood of the Saints and Martyrs. Hence, the saying of Jesus as He foresaw what was to come: "I bring not peace, but a sword," and "Blessed is he that loseth his life for my sake".

It was necessary to rouse the spirit of martyrdom that the age of darkness might be endured. This mystery of the blood cannot yet be fully explained, but it is most potent magic. Mme. Roland, in the French revolution, said, "Perhaps a willing victim may help to save the nation," in speaking of her own approaching death. Many have caught a glimpse of this strange law at the period of their martyrdom. And even the willing sacrifice of the armies for their nations has availed to stay the power of the fiends.

It has been necessary to teach the danger of hell, for these dangers are real to those who fell under the dominion of the demonic forces, lest they too should share the curse of damnation to the fires of the underworld. The book "Light on the Path" speaks of the Guardian Wall, which seeks to lift a little of the heavy Karma of the world and keep the dark forces from complete victory. All these things are significant.

Struggle for Light.—Now that the danger of the dark ages is past, man may emerge from blind devotion into the reasoned light of intelligence. But even so, man must not lose understanding of the great battle ground wherein he dwells and the need constantly to struggle for light, for right, for nobility and for self-sacrifice. It is not well that the forces of destruction be utterly ignored in one's own nature, or disaster will come and those things which permit the entry of evil must be guarded against—drugs, drink, and sex indulgence in a degrading form. Love in all aspects may be encouraged, so long as it sanctifies and teaches unselfishness and aspiration.

Police Force of the Heavens.—Out of the chaos will arise at last entities strong to serve and strong to save, fitted to rule over turbulent forces in the universe. They will have gained mastery over the destructive forces in life and in the planet, and may be sent without danger into all parts of the Solar Schemes. Their destiny will make them the police force of the heavens, sent wherever the destructive energy endangers harmonious evolution.

In this planet here, efforts should be made to harness some of the better elements, who are inclined to a destructive way of life, to the correction and curbing of crime. Later will be learned the necessity and value of this reordering of destructive force.

VII · THE INNER WORLDS

VII · THE INNER WORLDS

DEPARTMENTS OF WORK

Fauna and Flora.—There are many departments of work in the inner worlds. Some have to do with the changing fauna and flora. Scientific study is made of the effect these things have upon human evolution. Everything gives out its own magnetism and embodies certain definite forces in the System. When evolution demands a new human type, the vegetable and animal life surrounding it must be considered. It is significant that in America almost all forms of wild life except deer, foxes and birds are dying out. This is to modify the savage element in man. Even the deer and bears are tame and become park pets. In the future there will be less and less wild life, and the creatures will be cultivated as protected semi-pets for their usefulness.

Demonic Evolution.—Another department studies the line of demonic evolution, to see how the energies are used, controlled and co-ordinated in their own habitats. In this way it is hoped to learn how best to employ the demonic energies of man, those which he has gained from contact with that kingdom, and from the admixture of members of that kingdom. War has been the answer in the past, but cannot be that of the future. Another outlet must be found, to direct these energies constructively.

Racial Devas.—A third department which has much responsibility is that which deals with racial Devas, and racial genius. At this time, when the organization of the world must be achieved, modifications in all racial specializations must be made so that there may be, as it were, a common denominator of characteristics which will permit understanding, not suspicion. Hence, the modifications in clothes and customs in all races and the increase of uniformity.

Magic.—Another department has to do with magic. Here volunteers are trained to combat destructive elementals and to cleanse out centres of bad magnetism. This is a dangerous line of duty, similar to mine-sweeping in the war. The consequences may become disastrous at any moment, and disease, insanity and destruction may occur. Nevertheless, progress is being made.

Interplanetary Forces.—A very vital department is that connected with the distribution of interplanetary forces. These are gathered into reservoirs and stepped down, as by a transformer, according to the need. If a nation needs rousing or stirring or calming, these reservoirs are employed to drench the people like a pipe system of fire control. This department has only recently begun to be efficient, as it has taken a long time to teach any one how to handle these forces. It is one of the new departures of inner plane work, and it is hoped, will be useful in stabilizing conditions everywhere. Not only must the operatives know their work, how to store and release these forces, but there must be in each nation trained persons to act as distributing agents.

The Unfoldment of Powers

There are other departments of work. It is important that man not only realizes his possible control over the realms of the physical world, but begins to unfold the powers belonging to his true self and expressed only in fullness in his own kingdom in the inner worlds. His control of this planet is to relieve him from fear and rebellion bred by fear, to free him from the worship of the elemental gods. When a man knows himself safe from the elemental fears of death, of disease, of hunger, of violence, he is ready to develop in himself the powers of the spirit. His entire energies will not be devoted to sustaining life and to defeating dangers on the physical plane. He will no longer be a slave of tyrannical gods nor the puppet of unjust fate.

Methods of Organization

Testing of Volunteers.—Various efforts are being made to organize work effectively on the inner planes, and to prepare for organization on the physical. Many volunteers are being tried and tested for various roles. And many are found wanting. But the testing continues.

Work of the Deva Groups.—Through long ages preparation has been made, and various forces have been brought to bear upon mankind. The culmination is approaching. Certain groups of Devas have been given much added power—having earned it—and are preparing to subdue the destructive, elemental forces of the planet. Some of the Hierarchy, armed with the new electrical force from Sirius, and that recently unsealed on this earth, are planning a far-reaching campaign upon the demonic hosts loose on the planet. Both of these efforts must of necessity be somewhat slow of result. It is a titanic task and one that requires prolonged and intensive effort. It may be of interest to know more of the methods used.

Work of the Demon Groups.—In the case of the demonic groups, they are slowly being isolated into a smaller and smaller radius. Group after group of the more advanced egos are being freed from their assaults and insulated by a protecting veil of electrical matter through which the demonic influences cannot penetrate. This will gradually so purify the aura of these leading beings that they will trust each other and their people will trust them. The insidious sowings of suspicion and slander against the leaders will cease to avail. Naturally, however, as certain groups of humans escape the control of the demons, these will concentrate their energies more intensively on such as can be reached. Hence, the increase of crime, dope, insanity, and even turmoil, i.e., China and India and Russia. Just how to meet this has not been determined, but meanwhile a large and ever more dominating group of tested and proven souls are coming into incarnation. The solution may be found through them and their influence.

Ancient Elementals Destroyed.—The elemental forces provide a different problem. Some of the ancient elementals are being individually sought out and destroyed. These are mostly by-products of human evil-doing—like the sacrificial elementals one saw in the Yosemite. But a very real effort is being made to understand the source of the winds and storms in order to control these.

THE CEREMONIAL OF THE SPHERES

Deva Forms Are Built.—When the hour sounds for new effort, thousands who have been waiting rush forward to take advantage of the new down-pouring. They have not been able, perhaps, to share in the preparatory labours, but they can do their part as the new life pours down. Through music, rhythm and dance they share in the great ceremonials which form the etheric moulds for the conserving of force. Thus they help build the forms which the Devas fill. It is amazing what can be accomplished during the leadership of a wise occultist. By chants the volunteers tune up their vehicles until they are charged with power, then at a signal they pour the power thus gained out to the presiding official who in turn discharges it into the forms prepared. Here is a ceremonial similar to the church service.

Storages of Power.—There are, however, many other forms equally effective. Dance, under certain conditions, can be most stirring. The key of power lies in heightening the vibrations until the vehicles are intense and vibrating with great speed. This can be accomplished in various ways, best suited the temperament of the person or group. These storages of power are used in many ways in the ensuing months; for healing, for cleansing the planet, for inspiring the political leaders, for answers to prayers. Great groups of people apply for budgets of force for their work, just as heads of departments do here for money.

Occult Force Is Like Money.—This occult force is the money of the inner planes. It is probably a form of prana, universal energy, stored like grain against the hour of need, during the turn of the sun Northward when fresh force begins to flow for the use of the planet. One reason for establishing occult centres south of the Equator is to enable the solar forces to be stored at all times of the year. It may seem odd that geographical position should control the inner plane forces, but there is the magnetic centre of the earth

North of the Equator, and this affects many things. Also, the position of a person's physical body, geographically, determines the seasonal action of prana, for much of this work depends upon the use of the physical body as a matrix. Even at night the physical link is kept, and the body forces used.

MYSTERIES OF EGYPT

Practical Occultism.—The mysteries of Egypt not only gave deep and abstruse laws as to the inner worlds and the life after death, but the teaching was above all things concerned with practical occultism, the application of occult laws to daily life and the developing and unfolding of powers and faculties of immediate use to the state.

Magnetic Centres.—All the Hierophants wielded special powers which were designed to help in the development of the best of the race and to create centres within which they could carry on work of an occult nature for the state and thus definitely contribute to the peace, well-being and comfort of the nation. The Hierophants knew how to summon forth certain beneficent powers of nature. These they invoked to assist them in building powerful magnetic centres which repelled the general conditions of the planet and kept the undesirable elementals away.

This knowledge was in part a residue of the magic brought over from Atlantis, from the days of the City of the Golden Gates. Until the centre was established, it was essential to have in the land of Egypt only those who were powerless to make an opening for certain types of elementals.

Then when the ground and surrounding physical conditions had been perfected and prepared, a centre was established connecting up the inner worlds so that a perpetual funnel should act to carry down the forces. This was done usually through a temple or pyramid, which contained certain talismans or highly magnetized objects that constantly radiated force from high levels and acted as portals for the descent of power from the higher worlds. This sanctuary served a triple purpose. It constantly poured out power on the surrounding centre. It made it possible for those brought into it to have their vehicles worked upon and expanded. It made a suitable chamber of silence where seers could be taught specifically the occult lore and wisdom needed for the people and the nation.

Ring-Pass-Not.—The power of centre-building included the use of forces of an electrical and cleansing nature—like violet rays in church ceremony—destructive if not used wisely. It is the force which repels and kills when used too powerfully. It sets up an electrical current which shatters all impinging forces, and it acts as a ring-pass-not to undesirable elementals. It is, in fact, the same force which surrounds a Solar System and keeps out inharmonious influences and entities. Only those who have the pass-word—a mantramic word which sets their vehicles vibrating at a rate similar to the electrical current ringing the system—can enter.

Here one has the earliest origin of pass-words and words of power, and the control of reservoirs. Words of power set in motion certain vibrations which unloose the keystone of the portal of the reservoir and set the forces stored within flowing out. Usually there is a closing word unless the password looses a given and established amount. These power-

ful actinic forces were sealed for a long period during the
dark ages as too dangerous to permit to be in activity during the darkness of man's soul. Now again the power has
been restored and, as said elsewhere, it will destroy disease.
One form of it is electricity.

Training of Neophytes.—Within this magnetized field, it
was safe to train neophytes and to sensitize them so that
they could carry through not only the knowledge but the
powers of the inner planes. Their bodies were carefully
preserved from assault from elementals through the elec-
trically charged ring and could, therefore, be safely sensitized to a high degree. Some of the power vested in the
Hierophants was for the purpose of sensitizing vehicles.
This was the basis of the Initiations, and in the preliminary
tests it was found certain requisites of character alone
safeguarded the use of force. Courage above all, peaceable-
ness, control of passion in all forms and finally silence. The
training was strict, but the rewards were commensurate.
When passion had been controlled, marriage within the
ranks of neophytes was encouraged, and from the children
of these marriages the future neophytes were drawn. It gave
Egypt a race of singularly wise and holy priests and priest-
esses, who brought great knowledge to the nation. For not
only occult lore was taught, but science was studied at the
same time, medicine and herbs, astronomy, astrology, chem-
istry. For scientists entered the sanctuary and sought in holi-
est manner to have revealed more of the secrets of God.

Ceremonies of Sacrifice.—From these centres radiated
influences which kept the people from crime, which kept
the forces of nature in beneficent mood. When a crime
was committed it was realized that the whole nation was

endangered, and all members of the locality performed a penance to re-establish the balance of nature-forces which had been disturbed. To accomplish this certain ceremonies of purification were performed and sacrifices made to the elemental gods. It was recognized that crimes, especially of violence, permitted evil beings to flow through the rent made in the magnetic sheath of the nation. Repeated crime brought exile, the direst punishment in the eyes of patriotic Egyptians and with good reason, for health, wealth and peace flowed through the magnetized land of Chem.

GARDENS OF THE GREAT GOD

Let the spirit bathe in peace and dwell in tranquillity. Each day let the mind consider the serenity which guards the sanctuaries of the inner worlds, but which may be reached by all those who fulfill the prescribed requirements. These great fields of space where tranquillity dwells are the gardens of the Great God, where His wearied and troubled children may come to find refreshment of spirit jaded through the labours of the worldly day. Many souls cannot achieve these fields while in the body, but in the sleeping hours are guided there by compassionate guardian angels who have volunteered for this service. Some of the earth's children, who have learned while in the body to tread the ways of consciousness in the inner worlds, can achieve these planes in waking hours. Seek ye all this to do.

These pure oases of refreshment have been established at the request of some of the Holy Teachers who have come to assist in earth's redemption, that their devoted disciples might have strength to endure through the darkness of earth life.

These gardens of delight are dreamed of by many earnest souls—and have been the basis of the Paradises and Happy Hunting Grounds and Valhallas offered in all religions for the consolation of the virtuous who could never attain their reward upon earth during the period of its dominion by the dark powers. They can be reached without death by those who earnestly demand the right of entry, and the peace and the exquisite joy which dwell there may be brought back by these pilgrims for the refreshment of those themselves unable to achieve the goal. Many can touch the outer fringes when they contact what may be termed currents of happiness, but the power to penetrate these sanctuaries comes as the result of pain and anguish of mind, heart and spirit. More and more must humanity learn to journey there that it may continue to endure safely during these turbulent years of transition without the disaster of insanity which is the dire fate threatening the more sensitive and oppressed of the race.

First Ray Work

Now is the hour of peace. In the inner worlds the pendulum has swung past the low point of endeavour and there is rejoicing as the new forces begin to pour into the system now that the solstice is at hand. There is very strenuous effort during the months of the second half of the year. All that has grown and matured during the spring and summer months must be conserved, assorted and assimilated. It is like salvaging treasures that have been brought in by the high tide lest when it begins to turn it sweep back all it has brought forth. Then much preparation is made to take advantage of the new tide. Old refuse must be cleared away.

Volunteers must be trained and prepared, and the channels kept open that the new life may flow in smoothly and unbroken.

The preparation of the form is all first Ray work, and the hardest labours of those on this Ray come from July first on, especially from September twenty-first. For the year is really divided into three parts, the preparation, the flow and the assimilation; the last being the work of the Maha-Chohan, as he distributes the forces gathered into the appointed channels. But in the fall the plan of campaign is marked out, and the assistants trained for their posts. The reservoirs are cleansed and the forms built for conserving the new tides of life as they flow in. Reservoirs which have been too much depleted must be kept filled by volunteer efforts until the new life force flows in. It is arduous labour.

VIII · THE EVOLUTION OF VENUS

VIII · THE EVOLUTION OF VENUS

Venus—The Foster Mother of Earth

Relation of Venus and Earth.—When the word of doom was uttered, and the purpose of the plan diverted, certain cosmic adjustments were necessary, and certain members of the Solar Scheme were called upon for special service and assistance. Of those who volunteered, Venus and its wisest souls proved in this period to be the most useful, and into their hands was placed the governance of the planet, after a specified point of evolution. There is a special relation between Venus and Earth, for Venus has become the foster mother, and Earth the foster child.

Venus Evolves Through Wisdom.—Furthermore, Earth is carrying out on a lower level, and in more difficult conditions, some of the methods of evolution on Venus. Venus evolves through love—brotherly love. Earth evolves through passion—sex love. Venus achieves through wisdom. Earth can achieve only through intelligence, the lower phase of wisdom. Intellect alone can govern the forces of the vehicles and direct them into spiritual and constructive channels. There is ever a struggle going on between Venus and the play of the forces of wisdom and aspiration, which should have been the line of man's evolution, and Saturn, into whose kingdom—the world of material form man fell. Symbology has been much confused. Saturn rules dense form, and when man fell into his kingdom by error, he came under strange laws not suited to his nature. Sex love became materialistic, no longer a communion of souls, with the resulting uplift and service which comes from the interplay of spiritual love, the comradeship and assistance which results from the happy exchange of polarity—but lapsed into an animal-like struggle for supremacy, and a driving and intolerable physical urge that often brutalizes and degrades. This is the influence of Saturn working upon forces that do not belong to his realm.

Domination of Saturn.—It is the purpose of the leaders now to teach all humans to sublimate their love, and to seek to achieve that delicacy, union and friendship which comes from true communion. Each soul, ere he contact and hold true love, must conquer the domination of Saturn and the domination of sex—now a jealous, ruthless, cruel, intemperate and ill-judged force which has in it little of sanity and beauty. During courtship, before this force is too much roused, love touches something of the Venusian devotion, sacrifice, aspiration and beauty. Too often the consummation of marriage brings discord. Men have fallen again under the brutality and materialism of Saturn. Women, being more intuitive, are of their nature closer to Venus, and seek to lead men to that ennobling love.

Note that in India it was customary in the higher classes to forbid marriage in its complete phase until both had achieved complete control of passion. This teaching was based on the old law known to the Teachers of the race. There is much to study in this revelation, much that will explain the strange pain which love or other passion brings, and its inevitable penalty. For there is actually a Karmic penalty which results from falling under the sway of passion, a penalty of pain, physical or emotional. Hence the old teaching of celibacy.

The grip of the old elementals upon man's vehicles is easing. It may be that laws will change, but a certain amount of suffering must always stem from sex life which is not sublimated to the spiritual plane, to the tender rather than the passionate note, to self-sacrificing rather than exacting love.

OUR ADOPTION BY VENUS

Major Force of Planets.—In the starry vaults of Heaven are many types of Systems, with varying humanities—some trained for one purpose, some for another. The Logoi themselves vary in their methods, in their past, in their future purpose. Each System, however large, represents a centre and therefore a specialized power in the larger Cosmos. And even great groups of Systems in the end come under the classification of some major electric or magnetic powerhouse. There is, therefore, in any given planet a dominating character, a typical major force to which all others are subordinate. And power can only be transferred from one to another where there is similarity of major vibrations. This means only that one cannot tune in on vibrations to which one's radio does not respond.

The Great Man.—Now, it happens that although this planet is one of the lowest in some ways (not in point of density, however) it comes within the range—the tuning-in range—of a vast System. It is a tiny station in a particularly extended System, and can be reached, therefore, by many varied types of planets. That is one reason why so many visitors come, and so many experiments are made. At any rate, it has made it possible to invoke assistance from high and remote sources, which will probably greatly change the ultimate destiny of the planet. It was this peculiarity—that its range of vibration happened to enter the range of this vaster System and, as it were, made such unpleasant static—that first commanded the attention of some of the Mighty Rulers, and finally drew here the Great Man.

He understood that there were possibilities of salvage here, and set himself the task of repairing and tuning this faulty instrument. When the instrument had been repaired, he hoped to tune in on some powerful station which should drown out the discordant tunes played here, and teach the people to desire harmony and respond to it. It has been a titanic task to develop here the virtues needed to make response possible, but it has apparently been achieved. The great note needed was sacrifice. Hence the wars, the religious sacrifices, tithing, etc., which have taught men sacrifice. A very large part has been played through the development of the instinct of motherhood, with its infinite capacity for sacrifice. This instinct, once developed, appeared not only in women, but in men.

This planet, although one of the most disastrous as far as conditions go, is not one of the densest. In fact, it is considerably less dense than many others, since the vapour—the mantle of waters—was cast about it. It has been the mental warp, not the physical, which has brought such unhappy conditions.

The Great Mother of Waters.—In planets where only physical form is sought, far greater density exists, more like solid metal or stone, without earth or sea. And such intelligences as work there dwell within the planet, not on its surface. It was the mercy vouchsafed by the Great Mother of Waters which saved men from the terrible doom of sharing the inner realms with the demonic hosts.

Again one should remember that the original failure was not here, but elsewhere, and the rebellious group of fallen Angels was cast here for punishment and atonement. In every system there must be a breeding group and experimental station for the utterly untrained force of the demonic hosts. This planet was that training place in our Solar System, until converted to other uses.

Saturn and Venus.—Saturn is the ruler of this planet in its earlier form (Satan) and ever his malign influence must be met, endured and overcome. Venus is the planet of our adoption, the representative of the Great Mother in our System. It is to break the final hold of Saturn that the Great Lords are come.

Balance of Force.—A balance of forces is always necessary in every system. There must be stability, rhythm and activity, three types of force—negative, positive, balanced. And, therefore, there must be the abodes of demons, Devas, and humans, in all Systems. Demons are positive force; Devas, negative, and humans, balanced. Demons, destructive; Devas, constructive, and humans using both as need arises, and therefore intelligent directors and masters of both. But it is needful and customary to keep them separated, not as here all admixed.

THE FEMININE COUNTERPART OF KUMARAS

Centre of Human Consciousness.—Far removed from this planet is the centre of humanity's consciousness. There is the world of reality, the Kingdom of Heaven whence man came and to which he must return. More and more he must lift his consciousness from absorption in the details of daily life into a realization of that other sphere, and a conscious sharing of its powers. Since error has cast him, however, onto the physical body of the planet, he must not relinquish his grasp here, but must order and perfect physical plane conditions, ere the race is free to raise its consciousness beyond this sphere.

Wisdom—the Great Mother.—Yet wisely to orient their point of view to the purpose of life, and to gain clearer vision as to how to fulfill that purpose, the leaders must raise their consciousness to those sublime levels where alone wisdom dwells. "Great is Wisdom, and happy are those who seek her early," Solomon told us. For indeed Wisdom is embodied as a great Goddess who guards humanity and seeks to guide its erring footsteps into the paths of peace. She is come from Venus, the feminine counterpart of the Kumaras, to rule and lead humanity. *She* is the Great Mother. She exists in time and space, and she serves all humanity, but she knows that she will speak most clearly through her daughters, the daughters of Isis, the Great Mother. Committed into her care is all the sacred knowledge of the planet, and only as her servers gain her feet and envisage her powers can they reveal the sacred Wisdom to men.

She it is whom Egypt served. She it is whom some have seen in vision, the great foster-mother of the planet, who in her great compassion has come from Venus to instruct this race. Some of her most illumined followers she has brought with her to serve in temples: the seers, the sybils and the prophets. Some she has won from the race of men to serve at her altar and to testify to the truth. She it was who spoke through the temples of Egypt, and she it is whom some women are pledged to serve in this life, to reveal wisdom to the children of men; and to her feet the daughters of men must be led that they may learn their destiny, their powers and the labours entrusted to them—their divine estate.

VENUS SPECIALIZES IN WISDOM

There are many methods of evolution in various universes and the results vary greatly. Certain requirements apparently exist which must be completed just as there are required subjects for a university degree. Beyond these, however, a great variation and specialization is possible. The graduates of different Systems, therefore, have greatly varying powers.

Some Systems specialize in love, some in power, some in intelligence, corresponding to the varieties of development along the rays in our own System. This planet seems to be seeking a balance of the three.

Venus specializes in pure reason, in wisdom, a blend of love and intelligence. Mars is power only; Jupiter, love exclusively. Evolution on Mars is swift and terrible and painful. On Jupiter, it is pleasant but very, very slow. Neptune evolves through development and control of occult forces, while Mercury evolves through higher intellect and science.

IX · KUNDALINI

IX · KUNDALINI

THE MOON AND THE SUN

The sun and moon have occult relations to the earth besides their physical ones. The sun represents creative mind, and the moon, Kundalini, creative fire. The moon rouses sex. The sun intensifies the mind. Those who use the mind much must avoid sun. Those who use the emotions are benefited by sun and should avoid the moon. The sun works directly on the head centre, intensifying the cerebro-spinal system. The moon works through the solar plexus or navel, intensifying the glandular system. Men are romantic at night but they do not know why. It is the moon acting upon their physical functions.

The sun should be avoided during periods of great mental activity. It is less dangerous to women than to men, and corresponds somewhat to the magnetism of men in repleting a woman.

KUNDALINI IS THE BASIS OF INSTINCT

The trailing clouds of glory that envelop the planets are the vestures thrown over them by the Mother of Waters, who is the daughter of the Mother of Space. It is the inter-play between the fiery principles of Electricity and its sons, and the watery principles of Space and her daughters, that brings about manifestation. The play of Electricity upon the Mother stirs her into action and creative fire. Kundalini

155

responds, within the depths of space. Kundalini is fecundating matter.

Creative Power in Woman.—It is the creative power which is so strong in woman, and which gives her control over the elemental things of growth: flowers, children, animals, planted crops and gardens. It gives her control, also, over many of the destructive things of earth: pests, diseases, plagues. As a whole, women are less troubled by insects and vermin than men. It is Kundalini which is active at child-birth, when a woman feels herself in the grip of a cosmic force. The whole sympathetic system is the product of the action of Kundalini, as the cerebro-spinal is the product of the brain. The sympathetic system is not controlled by the brain, but by the solar plexus, with merely a secondary reaction on the brain. Kundalini is the basis of instinct, and only at individualization does the mind undertake to guide the personality through the brain.

Women are naturally sensitive to moods, feelings, and conditions about them. A woman, highly evolved mentally, sometimes becomes harder than men because her true nature has been submerged or overbalanced. The intense use of the brain has a tendency to denature a woman, to demagnetize her, until she loses her creative power or genius. Only as she learns to approach life in her own nature's way, can she achieve her destiny. The brain must ever be the servant, never the master of her life. The brain of the present day is so limited that only when supplemented by the faculties of instinct, vision and intuition can the truth as presented by the brain be anything but lop-sided. If woman will learn to interpret her apperceptions, life will be clarified.

Capacity and judgment are not dependent upon intellect

but upon innate understanding, and this woman has to a greater degree than man. She is more interested in living than in doing, more in persons than in building forms.

Fulfillment comes through vision, tempered by judgment, balanced by caution, and achieved through the blending of intuition and knowledge. For generations knowledge has been so limited that there was no near approach to justify intuition. That period passes, and knowledge now among men can soon build the links which will make intuition seem sane.

KUNDALINI IS EARTH-BORN

The aura of the Wind Spirits is blue. They evolve through power and action. The aura of the Fire Spirits is red-orange. They evolve through power and penetration or aspiration. The aura of the Earth Spirits is green. They evolve through endurance and strength and stability. The aura of the Water Spirits is yellow. They follow the hue of intellect or intelligence. They evolve through adaptability. These four lines are similar to the four Deva Temples of the book "Man." Each element has subdivisions of teaching, healing, building of the Kingdoms, vegetable, animal and mineral. So that one gets methods of healing which involve each of the four elements. This too will be understood later.

There are then the earth or mother forces, and the sun or father forces, which can be used. All powers of the body, of feeling and instinct, belong to the earth. Kundalini is earth-born and releases the powers latent in matter, and therefore in the vehicles of man. It is not a spiritual force, but a force latent in form. The sun forces are related to intelligence and act as the directing agents for the earth forces. Hence, if earth forces are too soon aroused until the intelligence has mastered its vehicles and gained cool direction from knowledge and experience, disaster may result. Power undirected by controlled intelligence in any department of life is dangerous.

X · SUMMARY

X · SUMMARY

SIGNS IN THE COSMIC SPHERES

When the signal comes, high in the Cosmic Spheres, this planet will be flooded with power. In advance, however, matters must be prepared here and receptacles made ready, so that the power when it comes shall benefit and not shatter. Nation by nation, the forms must be prepared, the people tempered, the ball started rolling in the right direction. There remains still much to be done.

Endure a little longer, ye faithful workers. When the signal comes for the releasing of this flood of power, the hour of the lightening of doom, the hour of salvation foretold of old, will be at hand. All will work with the most amazing speed. The impossible will be accomplished in a few years. In the new enthusiasm and joy, power will be given into competent hands, which will re-cast the face of the globe.

It has been foretold that slums will vanish, but more important there will be vast industrial armies with the discipline of soldiers, and the emotional enthusiasm of patriotism. These will be enrolled from all slums to re-order evil conditions, to destroy and to re-build, and the money will come from the ancient military taxes in every nation.

Through the enrollment, many criminals will be kept out of mischief, and crimes will be punished by enrolling the evil doers in some of the more arduous sections of labour. Crime will become a subject for jeering and ridicule, ever

161

potent against the emotional dramatic type which is prone
to crime. Penal colonies will be established for the truly
unfit, and great happy farms for the sub-normal and feeble-
minded—industrial schools which will be largely self-gov-
erned and, therefore, free (to a considerable degree) from
the danger of oppression.

Traveling inspectors will be established, of the finest
minds of the nation, organized for volunteer work, to supervise the re-claiming of backward places and districts. They
will turn their magnificent minds to organizing, educating
and industrializing groups which are backward, in all parts
of the world.

Through the international office, reports can be made
and plans matured for which volunteers in each nation will
be called. Under the governing representative of each nation
on the Board, recommendations will be made which will
have all the weight of law.

The organization of this program will be carried out,
not by diplomats or officials, but by industrial boards made
up of the great industrial minds of each nation, who will
study how to make communities self-supporting and efficient,
and who will have at their hand vast resources of capital for
unfolding and developing these communities. Industrial co-
operation on a large scale will come. A man desiring to open
up a new business will refer to a chamber of commerce
which will present statistics and make recommendations.
The jobs will be assigned somewhat as in a play, as far as
possible only a certain number of one kind of store to a
given population.

None of this could be possible were it not for the new
idealism and enthusiasm, due to the new down-pouring of

power—the true Coming in a real sense—distributed among millions.

THE WHEEL OF CHANGE

The wheel of change controls all evolutions and all manifestation. Seasons, day and night, dark and light, cold and heat, attraction and repulsion, are ever manifesting their influences in all spheres, in all worlds, in all Systems. Growth and life are cyclic. In all things there is birth, growth, fulfillment and decay.

Birth.—Birth is aggressive. The forces are centripetal, selfish, self-centered. Gradually, as life continues, the force changes from centripetal to centrifugal, and the spiritual aspect which gives forth, not takes in, comes into play. Then develops the law of sacrifice, the law of spiritual adjustment, whereby the forces gathered in during the aggressive years are returned in full measure, ripened, increased and beautified to the universe.

The Middle Period.—In the middle period comes the balance, and man's success in any given life is judged by his capacity to swing over fully to the other pole. How much does he give? How much has he garnered? How will he use it? It has been said that the latter years of a man's life determine his next life. This is because of the law that he is judged only after the change of balance and polarity has taken place. Before that he is accumulating, and he is unready to begin his return of goods gathered once more to the universal store.

Mature Years.—That middle period of balance is the danger point in the life. It is a tearing and wrenching of consciousness that takes place, a violent adjustment, a spiritual birth. Many fail at this time. They reach back when the world is slipping from them, to grasp more of its gifts. Then it is that men and women alike cry out for their vanishing youth. Men reach out to young women for romance, glamour, passion, all the things of the aggressive arc of personal demand. Women do likewise in some measure, or become hysterical, morose, despairing. Yet the pendulum must swing, and those who grasp at personal happiness after the allotted years, reap misery and failure. For the Dharma, the duty, the purpose of mature years is voluntary service and sacrifice. That which applies to one human life, applies also to every other evolutionary arc. This planet is just emerging from the struggle of middle life into maturity from the ages of anguish to the age of peace, of giving, not taking.

Planetary and Solar Life.—In planetary life, when the middle point is past, the planet ceases to draw from the Solar System, but on the other hand begins to pour back its measures of spiritual essence, garnered in the days when it was young and verdant. In Solar Systems, the same is true, and the work and achievement is judged only by what is accomplished after the middle period. In almost all cases —human, planetary, solar—there is need of help during the crucial turning point. It is to this point that religions were especially directed. It is towards a happy issue of this period that volunteers came to troubled planets and Solar Systems.

THE INTERSTELLAR REGIONS—
LIMBO OF FORGOTTEN THINGS

Ocean Bed of Space.—The interstellar regions are filled with many various vibrations and ancient accumulations from dead planets and refuse from living ones. It is the ocean bed of space where ancient wrecks gather, and discarded materials from many sources drift about.

Driftwood of Forgotten Evolutions.—Here is the driftwood of many strange, forgotten evolutions, and the wrack and wreck of forgotten planets. When dying or dead planets finally break apart, their remains, in broken fragments, drift into the great cosmic ocean, and there await the day of cosmic disintegration. This cosmic ocean is situated in the centre of our saucer-shaped cosmos, and although universes may sprinkle it as islands do the sea, it is the lowest point of magnetic polarity, and it is here that those things repulsed by living planets gather. Many comets and meteorites finally end here, and it is here that the refuse of planets gather. It is the limbo of forgotten things, awaiting the day of final disintegration, when the universe retires into darkness.

Occasional lost and exiled souls drift there, like beachcombers awaiting cosmic death. And it is from this place that volunteers for desperate and hopeless missions are recruited, to give them a final chance at redemption. Many came to this planet when its Overlord laid aside his authority and left his kingdom a prey to invasion. Later barriers were raised to prevent further incursion, but in the limbo of space, wastrel bands of exiled entities drift about, and occasionally attack or seek to find foothold in some weaker planet.

Disintegration of Planets.—There are great battles fought between the hosts of light and the hosts of darkness, who come to assault a planet and who sometimes conquer. Occasionally when this occurs, the Overlords disintegrate the planet and rescue the worthy members. This happened to the Asteroids. A similar minor case was the destroying of Atlantis at the time of the great flood, and the rescue of the deserving, to establish a new race. These invading hordes take possession of the bodies of a race, if they are successful, and drive out the original inhabitants. It is a kind of wholesale obsession, and became successful in Germany. Such things can happen only under certain conditions where for some reason a planet is deprived of its natural protection. But there are indeed great battles in heaven for the possession of new lands. Be it remembered that spiritual wickedness in high places is mentioned in the Bible.

EPILOGUE

EPILOGUE

RENUNCIATION

From the throes of agony shall arise power, from the darkness shall come light, from renunciation shall come peace. *Only* through renunciation can come peace. Many are not yet ready for peace. Its very stillness, its very quiet disturbs them, for they yearn for the turbulence of emotional and astral life. They need the coarse vibrations of the lower vehicles to be conscious of the pulse of life. The more delicate and etherial play of consciousness which comes in music, beauty, art, poetry, friendship cannot satisfy them. Yet these are some of the gifts vouchsafed by peace.

When the soul has passed through broken and troubled waters, when pain and anguish and agony of mind have done their work, he is ready to turn away from turmoil at any price, and to seek peace. Then is he ready to enter the spiritual life; then only can he value and appreciate it. Earlier it would have been unsatisfying. For Heaven is not in the satisfaction of the senses. It is, on the contrary, in the starvation of the senses, and the satisfaction of the spirit. Many primitive souls cannot enter Heaven consciously, even after death, for they have as yet no capacity for enjoyment of those things which heaven offers.

They have not unfurled the pinions of the spirit wherewith to soar into the realms of God. They are still earthbound. For these have been made the earth-born Paradises

which are established in the astral worlds as playgrounds
for the child souls of the race. Not here can heavenly joys
be found—not here, but in that realm where man reveals
his true divinity, his radiant Augoeides. For this, when man
shall know himself divine and display that divinity in all its
brilliant panoply of spiritual power—for this alone is all
our long and anguished pilgrimage through eons upon eons
of time. To learn slowly to spread the pinions of the spirit
is evolution through grosser matter undertaken. This end
alone is worthy of achievement. This end alone brings peace.
This is the goal of all humanity, the fulfilment of God's
plan for man.

TRAVAILS OF THE SOUL

The travails of the soul are many on this strange planet,
not only for the humans who dwell here, but even those who
have but linked themselves to it for a purpose. Throughout
its stormy history, there has been confusion and doubt,
terror and disobedience and troubled hours for the souls
who sojourned here. A strange law rules which requires
obedience of the rebellious and rebellion in the obedient, as
it moves in varying cycles.

It is indeed a narrow path which must be trodden here,
ere man may escape his doom. Only a tempered soul, wise
and intelligent, controlled and kindly, may at last emerge
into freedom. The strong souls are beaten and buffeted to
temper them and the weak souls are beaten and tormented
to rouse them, for only the blend of strength and submission,
of wisdom and obedience, of understanding and power can
at last find the key to liberation. Peace. Let not the storm of
the past wash over the vessel of the present.

The Way of Service

The way of service is hard. Within the cell of flesh, the spirit pines. Yet so only can at last the butterfly emerge from the chrysalis. There is a period of intolerable discomfort before the latent energy is roused in the sleeping and dormant creature within its transparent shell. At last the discomfort becomes so great that it can no longer be borne, and the creature, grown to full size and conscious only of its cramped surroundings, begins to force back the encircling bonds, and ruptures its shell. So with man. At last the bondage of life becomes unbearable and he bursts from it, a liberated soul. The messengers who come are but voices preparing the mind for this supreme effort, warning man that he is imprisoned, and foretelling the need for liberation in the ultimate hour. So must nature whisper to the crawling caterpillar, ere it abandons its life upon the surface of the earth, and seeks for the sleep which shall bring re-birth.

Pioneers of the Race

So you who are pioneers of the race perform your greatest service when you blaze the trail, when you achieve, and from your serenity, anguish-born, inspire others to do likewise. How long, oh men, how long must you continue the sport of elemental forces which tear and rend you uncontrolled? How long must ye fall—a plaything of the lower gods—at the mercy of the elements of anger, jealousy, fear, greed and pride? The lower gods, the lords of the physical world, are the gaolers of mankind; theirs the sport to see how far their powers can control and guide these divine visitors, how long they can control and master the Sons of Light.

Rebellion is needed, rebellion against the domination of the elemental forces—the control by the Lords of the lower world—for man's dominion is not here. This is the plane of animals, and the Lords of the planet are the guides and guardians of the lower kingdoms. Only because of man's need for an animal body did he come under their dominion. Now he must arise and know himself not animal, but divine. Now must he seek the Lord of his own world, where he can unfold his god-like powers. If once he can understand that this world is not his, that his destiny is not to be dominated by earth-born forces, active in order to build the lower kingdoms, that he is but a sojourner here to gain control of certain forces. and vehicles for his future purposes, he will break away from this lower consciousness and know himself for what he is, a child of Light.

Each Man Himself the Path

In the many channels through which flow the forces of the higher worlds, there is opportunity for variety. Each man is himself the path. Each leader blazes the way for that small group of kindred souls who can follow in his steps, and leaves shining an ideal of love, service in action, to inspire thousands; and prepares them to aspire to find their own trails to the distant goal.

In every generation a few achieve, a few find the key to the labyrinth and go forth, carrying with them close companions who through repeated associations have learned to share their viewpoint and their consciousness. And each leaves the fragrance of a sacrificial life and each

leaves the record of his own path to God. And each re-
lieves a trifle the intolerable burden cast upon the planet
by the original error.

Peace. Peace, compassion and purity.

Frankincense and Myrrh

Frankincense and myrrh are offered the Teachers of
the world, lest they fail of their high destiny. Frankincense is the symbol of the benediction of the spirit; myrrh,
of the sacrifice of the flesh. These two always surround
the life of the spiritual teacher until the supreme sacrifice
is made and the power of the spirit transcends the anguished flesh—triumphant.

The Rhythms of the Spheres

The swinging rhythms of the spheres go by, and singing melody chimes in their wake.

The worlds are full of sound and glory, and the chasm
of blue space is filled with splendid harmony. A pageantry
of sound and colour is our firmament for those whose
ears and eyes can hear and see.

The seven sounds of song are cycles in a vaster symphony, and singing choirs chant from sphere to sphere
resounding chords that speak the Word of God for each
and every sphere its name, God-given ere the worlds
began.

Attune to these great harmonies and every atom becomes vibrant life and power and joy, and carries health.

Attune to these great singing choirs, and the Will and
Plan of God must be revealed.

Peace. No more.

CPSIA information can be obtained
at www.ICGtesting.com
Printed in the USA
LVHW03s0249111018
593107LV00003B/1154/P

9 781163 140611